THE VIOLENCE POTENTIAL

IN OUR SOCIETY TODAY

ERNEST PECCI, M.D.

PAVIOR PUBLISHING
WALNUT CREEK, CALIFORNIA

First Edition 1994

Published in the United States By

Pavior Publishing
2910 Camino Diablo, Suite 100
Walnut Creek, CA 94596

Copyright © 1994 by Ernest Pecci, M.D.

Cover and Typography by Edward Sheppie

Library of Congress No. 94-67782
ISBN 0-9642637-2-6

Table of Contents

INTRODUCTION

CHAPTER 1. ENVIRONMENTAL BOUNDARIES • 1
SETTING LIMITS

CHAPTER 2. THE INCREASE IN AGGRESSIVE BEHAVIOR
AND VIOLENCE • 15
THE BIOLOGICAL ROOTS OF ANGER
GENETIC PREDISPOSITION TO VIOLENT BEHAVIOR

CHAPTER 3. BONDING AND ROLE CONFUSION • 27

CHAPTER 4. POWER STRUGGLES • 33
SURVIVAL QUESTIONS

CHAPTER 5. CRAZYMAKING • 41
THE GROWTH OF STREET GANGS

CHAPTER 6. THE PECKING ORDER • 49
DOMINANT BEHAVIOR AND THE PECKING ORDER
WOMEN AND FAMILY VIOLENCE

CHAPTER 7. THE WILL-TO-POWER AND
THE WILL-TO-SERVE • 63
THE SERVITUDE TRAP
THE POLITICS OF OBEDIENCE

CHAPTER 8. THE PERFORMANCE TRAP • 73
FLOWER CHILDREN OF THE 60's
THE ESTABLISHMENT TRAP
THE WELFARE TRAP
THE RETIREMENT TRAP

CHAPTER 9.   THE MANAGEMENT OF JUVENILE
              DELINQUENTS • 87

CHAPTER 10.   EVALUATING THE MOTIVES FOR
              DISRUPTIVE BEHAVIOR • 99
              AGGRESSIVE PATTERNS ARE LINKED TO PLAY
              DEFENSIVE PATTERNS ARE LINKED TO VIOLENCE
              HOW THE MIND INFLUENCES ANGER
              FREUD'S THEORY ON VIOLENCE
              LEARNED HELPLESSNESS AND DEPRESSION

CHAPTER 11.   HOW THE BRAIN RESPONDS
              TO THE ENVIROMENT • 107
              THE FIVE MAJOR AREAS OF THE BRAIN
              CHRONIC STRESS SYNDROME

CHAPTER 12.   ASSESSING VIOLENCE POTENTIAL • 123
              VIOLENCE IS A LEARNED BEHAVIOR
              THE ANGER-TO-VIOLENCE STAGES
              STRESS-RELATED VIOLENCE
              ASSESS YOUR OWN VIOLENCE POTENTIAL

CHAPTER 13.   THE DISTINCTION BETWEEN AGGRESSIVE
              AND VIOLENT BEHAVIOR • 133
              SOCIALLY CONDONED AGGRESSION
              CHART OF CHARACTERISTIC DIFFERENCES
              AGGRESSION OR VIOLENCE QUESTIONS AND ANSWERS

CHAPTER 14.   BEYOND THE PECKING ORDER • 149

POSTSCRIPT   REFLECTIONS UPON THE GROWING VISION
              OF PSYCHOLOGY TOWARD A BROADER CONCEPT
              OF THE HUMAN MIND • 159

Introduction

Much research has been done to examine the many variables which determine human behavior. I have found that the understanding of behavior can be immensely simplified by understanding a few basic principles governing the behavior of social animals, and especially the dog.

I have had a long thirty-year friendship with an experienced dog trainer, William Meisterfeld, who has a kennel in Petaluma, California. For years I was impressed by his ability to take vicious dogs, and over a relatively small number of weeks convert them into friendly and obedient pets. I wondered if what he was doing could be applied to the raising of children since much of my practice, then, consisted of hyperaggressive and rebellious children.

He began to refer the dog owners to me because we observed that these owners were having the same problems with their own children as they were having with their pet dogs. They all complained of having "no control" over their children's behavior. Out of my conversations with Mr. Meisterfeld, I found that I could simplify the numerous theories and massive literature on child rearing and training into a few basic principles that work with consistent and dramatic effectiveness.

1

Dogs provide an ideal prototype for the study of behavior in humans because they, like humans, are genetically social animals. Equally important, dogs are unique in their willingness to seek a bond of servitude with humans as strongly as with members of their own species. This trait makes them analogous to young children, at least in all the essential ways in which we need to understand the effects of early environmental conditioning. It especially highlights the influence of different styles of training and discipline upon behavior.

The word "discipline" has negative connotations for most people, because in their own childhood it was often associated with suppression or control. Discipline, as used here, is not equated with punishment, coercion, or suppression. These actions are all measures resorted to by an autocratic authority figure when discipline has failed. These, too, ultimately fail in their goal. Although initially such actions may gain outward compliance, they promote resentment, rebellion, or passive-aggressive resistance through escapism or apathy. The proper exercise of discipline is essential for teaching a young child how to modulate his impulses and to meet challenges and expectations with greater and greater levels of mastery, so important for developing a positive self-concept.

Since most communication between young children and parents is non-verbal (actions and tone of voice carry more impact than words), we can find a number of parallels between children's behavioral responses and the behavior of puppy dogs to an authority figure. If this comparison appears to be an oversimplification, then all the better. Too often, children are treated as if they are tiny adults.

On the contrary, children are bewildered, confused,

in awe of adults and totally unable to comprehend adult motives. They cannot reason the way adults do because their frontal lobes, the reasoning part of their brains, is incompletely developed until after five years of age.

What children experience primarily is the intense need to be loved and to be found acceptable by their god-like caretakers. Their hypnotic-like suggestibility and susceptibility to the emotions of their parents gives to the parents a level of power over them that is unequaled in any other human relationship. Most parents are unaware of their power and commonly misuse it by careless, critical, harsh, or impatient rough handling, which inflicts deep emotional wounds on the psyche of the child.

The relationship of a child to his parents necessarily changes as he evolves through the various developmental stages from total dependence, to imitation and identification and, finally, to autonomy and independence. It is important for parents to understand the nature of their power to mold the behavior and self-image of their child, and to understand when to make a shift in their mode of discipline and their relationship to the child as he matures.

In contrast, the relationship of a pet, such as a dog, to its owner remains relatively constant throughout its lifetime. Nevertheless, in my twenty-five years as a child psychiatrist, during which I consulted with countless parents, teachers, social workers, and juvenile authorities, I have arrived at this dramatic realization: the early training and discipline of a young child up to the age of four or five years must follow the same basic principles as those used by experienced dog trainers who train with mutual respect. A full understanding of the implications of this statement can remove the mystique from child-rearing and bring clear answers to the often asked question: "Where did I go wrong?"

During his early years, the child's understanding of himself and of the world is limited, and even his capacity to understand complex relationships does not come until much later. The child cannot possibly understand adult motives or reasons for requiring certain behaviors. Neither can he be expected to understand the "why's" of his own emotions and behavior.

It is a period when he needs help developing control over his feelings and impulses. His ability to postpone gratification is limited, and his tolerance for frustration is minimal. He is dependent upon you, and upon your manner of seeing and responding to him, for a sense of self. At every moment of your relating or not relating, you are telling him who he* is.

During the period of early training, the child is disciplined to behave according to the rules and limits that you have decided are important, and which you have established within the given environment.

Discipline, to be effective, must be established upon a basis of mutual respect and trust, and requires minimal or no physical enforcement. The average parents have no idea how much influence they really have over their children's behavior and how they, themselves, inadvertently condition their children into the patterns of rebellion and defiance of which they complain. Early training practices establish the foundation for all future communication between parent and child.

*The word "he" is used in the same text as an impersonal pronoun applying equally to both male and female.

It is the goal of this book: 1) to educate the public to become more aware of the responsibility we have in shaping the self-concept and behavioral habits of our children; 2) to identify some of the destructive consequences of the self-serving practices of people in authority, practices which threaten the survival of our democratic society; and 3) to modify the unrealistic expectations for performance in our culture that are leading us further and further away from our essential nature as spiritual beings. With this loss of identity comes jealousy, a sense of lack, competition, and finally, the fear and rage of an animal under attack in a potentially hostile environment.

Chapter One

Environmental Boundaries

From infancy, a child begins to learn about himself and about the material world through his play. It takes up to three years for a child to comprehend fully the concepts of "in" and "out," "big" and "small," "up" and "down," and the permanence of material substances when they are out of sight. Gradually, through trial and error, he learns his limitations in regard to manipulating the material world. He also learns through parental admonitions that there are things he can touch and things he must not touch, although the reasons are not always clear.

In a similar fashion the child gradually comes to terms with the real and dictated limits of his immediate environment. The healthy child is filled with a natural impulse to explore, examine, interact with, and experience new frontiers in his world of wonderment. With each limit comes a sense of frustration.

Not recognizing his mortality, he will exercise every sense organ and include fingers and mouth to explore the surfaces of every colorful object within his reach. Moving objects fascinate him, and he is even more delighted by his ability to move, spin, or pile them into configurations of his own choosing. This gives him his first sense of power.

There is also the sensory component of his makeup, which seeks constant stimulation. If, in his process of discovery, he takes a mild tumble, or rolls, spins, or swings, after a momentary startle and a reassessment of his intactness, he will take delight in repeating the motor movements over and over again to keep his inner gyro spinning.

But, again, a limit is eventually set to the boundaries of his three-dimensional world. A wise parent will child-proof an area of the house to minimize the repetitive "no" which abruptly puts a stop to the natural flow of the seeking of new experiences. A series of repeated "no's" at any age can lead to a buildup of frustration, which can lead to a temper tantrum.

A temper tantrum is the result of a child's loss of control over his frustration at being repeatedly blocked in the middle of an intended action. Thus, early environmental conditioning is centered upon the core concept of setting limits. How this is done has a powerful impact upon both the child's security and his self-concept.

Setting Limits

It's as basic as "yes" and "no." An environment in which the "yes's" and the "no's" are predictable and consistent is a safe environment. When the "yes's" and "no's" are inconsistent and the "no's" harshly imposed, there is insecurity, resentment, and the urge to rebel.

As the child repeatedly tests the real and the arbitrary limits placed upon his movements, if these limits remain reasonably expansive and consistent he will gradually accept and even experience a sense of safety within a finite area that he now sees as "his ego space." Out of this perception a sense of territoriality arises. This is now his realm, and he may resent other children violating this space unless he can attain some type of dominance over them. Parents who inconsistently contract and expand the child's "world-space" foster a reaction of rebellion and defiance, or insecurity and fear.

In both animals and children there comes a sense of security in knowing one's boundaries. In a real sense, having boundaries means having a predictable and safe space where freedom of movement is relatively unlimited. A sense of personal possession is attached to the objects within that space.

The lack of a well-defined boundary fosters a sense of being untethered or uncared for and, with this, a feeling of insecurity. It is not unusual for a child to provoke a spanking from a parent in order to elicit a sense of caring and to force an authority figure to define the child's behavioral boundaries. Children in therapy have commented to me: "My parents don't care what time I come home or where I go—they just don't care about me. John's parents punish him because they care."

A child's boundaries must gradually expand as he advances to the role of adult. Setting clear and consistent emotional and physical limits during this process of expansion is essential to fostering healthy growth and teaching respect for the territorial space of others.

There is a right way and a wrong way to set limits. Limit-setting necessitates a prior decision on your part as to which behaviors will be tolerated and which will not be permitted. Then there must be consistent communication of these limits by both word and action, before and during the times that these limits are being tested by your child, student, or whomsoever you have the responsibility to supervise, and it is a certainty that limits will be tested.

Keep in mind that the healthiest environment you can create is the one that imposes the fewest "no's" and "don'ts." This includes keeping to a minimum the likelihood of the child's being hurt, or articles being damaged, or that an embarrassing or upsetting mess will be made of the setting without your constant interference and control of the situation.

In the case of a young child, you must realize that young children have only minimal control over their own behavior. The immediate environment may be too threatening, forbidden objects too seductive, the restrictions too frustrating, or the expectations of "good" behavior too unrealistic. An understanding of the energy that is being expressed by a particular behavior, i.e., curiosity, excitement, etc., is necessary to appropriately encourage such behavior or to terminate it. This means being alert to the buildup of tension so as to defuse or re-channel it while it is still easily manageable. Interruption of the natural flow of any intent or expression in midstream is guaranteed to provoke inner rage.

Parents often do not realize how important a child's territorial space is to him and so, inadvertently, frequently violate it, causing "unexplainable" fits of temper. For example, the introduction of a new baby into the home has to be done with a sense of understanding how this can provoke a high level of anxiety and resentment in the child.

Also, witness how differently children relate to a friend, depending upon whether that friend is visiting his house or he is visiting theirs. There is a general pattern in pre-pubescent boys and girls (ages 10–13) to be more passive, obliging, and willing to "fit in" when at the home of a playmate.

Conversely, when they are the host/hostess in their own home they set the tone, direct the activities, and generally take on the airs of the "person in charge." I observed this in my own son, who was somewhat reticent and shy during his early teens in the company of his friends when in their homes, but would take on a noticeably dominant attitude when his friends came to visit to play computer games on his turf.

Even relatively restricting limits will be accepted as providing a safe or cozy home base without provoking resentment or resistance, depending upon how those limits were set. If they are not set with the energy of caring and respect, then children will resent and rebel against those limits, as does a prisoner to his prison cell.

Every encounter with a child gives him a message of acceptance or rejection, and tone of voice is more important than the words used. The child is hypersensitive to everything you say as an indication of whether or not you are happy over his having been born. When parents place their child in a crib or in an enclosed outdoor area to get them out of the way, to be free from them, the child receives "don't exist" messages. This perception arouses his survival instincts and may cause him to whimper or howl until he receives some kind of attention, even if it is negative attention, which is better than none.

If the limit-setter is not respected in the home, there will be no respect for limit-setting done by the authorities that control the greater society. Without mutual respect and caring, constant force is needed to maintain territorial limits.

We see this among neighboring countries everywhere in the world today. Humans have an innate need for a safe haven, a home base, a place they can call their own to return to after traveling, exploring, or fighting a war. Thus, we have factions, cliques, fraternities, and countries fighting for their territorial boundaries.

An example of the result of disrespect for any outside authority to establish territorial boundaries is the increasing tendency of youth to regress atavistically back to pack behavior, as seen in the street gangs of most major cities, where territorial boundaries are protected with whatever violence is necessary.

Civilization, by its definition, implies a structure with a socializing veneer that peacefully maintains territorial boundaries. This is especially true within the confines of a homogenous culture, and when the man of each household has a significant place and role in the sustaining of that culture. In "polite society" the majority of citizens willingly conform to social pressures that temper aggressive intrusions into another person's boundaries. However, as the social structure weakens, so too does its protective socializing restraint upon aggression and violence.

While we must be cautious as to the danger of directly comparing human behavior to animal behavior, there are some suggestive examples that help give insight into human innate propensities under particularly stressful environmental conditions. Dr. Frederick

Goodwin, Director of the National Institute of Mental Health, sees some noteworthy parallels between the violent behavior of young male rhesus monkeys and that of young, male human beings.

Goodwin proposes that the rise of inner-city violence might be the result of a loss of "civilizing" social factors comparable to those in a monkey society that usually keep the adolescent male's naturally violent behavior in check. Studies show that when young males leave the restraining social fabric of a monkey troop, as they do at a key stage in their lives, some become hyperaggressive, and even murderous. Goodwin suggests that the loss of structure in human society might be similarly responsible for the upsurge in urban violence.

This suggestion makes sense if we consider that we are inherently social beings, and our sense of security is gained only through bonding with a caring and supportive group. Without this bonding we suffer fear, alienation, and a survival-of-the-fittest mentality that can lead to cruelty in the name of self-defense.

Chapter Two

The Increase in Aggressive Behavior and Violence

Violence and the fear of violence have become major concerns of every citizen of this country today. Supposedly, in the most technologically advanced and humane culture on the planet, few of our public parks and streets are safe at night. As the statistics for rape and murder spiral upward yearly, significantly, so do the incidents of vicious attacks within the family by even the family dog, a phenomenon which was almost unheard of in the past.

Are we creating the potential for violence within our young, or has our civilization become too complex to put constraints upon the natural propensity for violence that was always there?

Every day we read in the newspapers new appeals to curb violence by winning the war against drugs, by establishing gun control laws, and by building more prisons and imposing tougher penalties on criminals. None of the above, even if carried out to a high degree of success, will significantly reduce violence. We hear that poverty, prejudice, stress, and job frustration all contribute to violence. But this is only partly true. Otherwise, why was violence such a rare event during the Great Depression of the 1930's when I was growing up?

I remember when I was ten years old how a sense-less rape and murder in the Boston suburb, where I was raised, created a wave of shock that lasted for many weeks, even after the young man was appre-hended. Today, and especially in the major cities, incidents of rape and murder have become so common-place that they barely make the news of the day on the front page.

Interestingly, dog viciousness against children has gained increasing attention. We can learn a lot from this trend because viciousness in dogs and violence in humans have common roots. Guns, drugs, and poverty have little to do with it. Surely, defanging a dog will reduce his potency, but will not cure the problem. The problem lies in the fact that we are breeding violence in our children and our young adults faster than we can control it by counter-punitive means.

During my years of working as a psychiatrist in the California Youth Authority, I became intrigued by the issue of violence. I saw hundreds of teenagers incarcer-ated for senseless crimes. Drugs and weapons were often involved, and most of these teens came from poor neighborhoods. Yet, how many people in this country have taken drugs and not felt the urge for violence? How many people have access to guns or knives with-out the compulsion to use them? I, myself, was raised in poverty all through the Depression, and the thought of a violent act of any kind never came into my head.

One of the reasons for so much controversy around the causes and the control of violence is a tendency to link anger, frustration, and violence together in one package, whereas they are only indirectly linked. *Violence is a learned or environmentally conditioned behavior that can*

be eliminated through proper rearing practices with children.
Before I review the thinking process by which I and other researchers in the field are arriving at this conclusion, I want to point out that it is strongly validated by anthropologists who have noted that an isolated island population of totally passive and peaceful tribal people can be transformed into a warlike, violent population within two generations.

At this point, let us propose a basic definition of violence: *Violence is excessive use of force directed toward a target victim with the intent to inflict pain and suffering.* "Intent" is the key word here. Is the intent survival, i.e., self-protection; is the intent to obtain food; is it for sport; or is it to inflict revenge for a past act of aggression?

The motives for violence may be complex and the emotions that accompany it such as anger, fear, frustration, etc., vary widely. More often we are shocked at the "cold-blooded" nature of violence, after which the perpetrator shows relatively little guilt or remorse.

Courts of law seek mitigating circumstances such as drugs, "uncontrollable impulse," provocation, self-defense, and "temporary insanity" to forgive acts of violence. However, we know that schizophrenics and those labelled legally insane are no more prone to violence than is the general population. Diabetics and people suffering from hypoglycemia (albeit the famous Twinkie case, where Dan White was given a light sentence for murdering the mayor and a supervisor because he ate a pastry beforehand) do not become violent. The average person who imbibes alcohol or who takes LSD does not automatically behave violently.

Generally, the perpetrator of violence feels little or no remorse for his actions because those actions are the result of a learned behavior that he is convinced inwardly was justifiable under the circumstances. Perpetrators of violence are more likely to become exhilarated at the retelling of their perpetrations and, at best, feign remorse when in group therapy they are confronted with the suffering of their victims.

Dozens of young men whom I interviewed, who had committed senseless violence, and most of whom were otherwise friendly and likable in a prison setting, all recount in different terms their experience of excitement and exhilaration (the adrenal rush described in greater detail later), and the sense of personal power accompanied by a gratifying release of pent-up rage, hurt, and frustration that brings with it a lingering "high" that can be addictive, like cocaine.

It must be stated clearly: *Violent behavior is highly addictive in both humans and animals.* This fact helps to explain why the greatest predictor of violent behavior is a previous history of violence. This principle also applies to violence against one's own body. Even relatively minimal acts of violence against the self, such as wrist cutting in a suicidal gesture, can bring an experience of stimulation coupled with a release of emotional pain so that self-mutilation might thereafter become an impulsive tendency.

There is a large population of otherwise non-violent self-mutilators in the general population, who often call themselves, "cutters," most of whom were emotionally or sexually abused as children. The relief they experience from the cutting provides an example of how some people receive pleasure from pain. This includes pain inflicted upon themselves or pain inflicted upon a victim. I interviewed a youthful murderer once, who confided that cutting his victim's throat was a way of releasing the tension in his own throat.

There is no denying the powerful imprinting that being the object of violence or sexual abuse has upon a young child. The majority of child molesters were, themselves, molested as children. One young man I interviewed told me that when he was six years of age he was kidnapped and sexually molested by an 18-year-old boy. When he himself reached the age of 18, he felt compelled to molest a six-year-old boy, the crime for which he had been incarcerated.

Anger, hostility, and aggression are not synonymous with violence. Some aggression is healthy and perhaps necessary as a motivating factor, when properly channeled, to accept challenges and to gain mastery through difficult accomplishments.

Some anger in the course of everyday frustrations is unavoidable, but rarely leads to violence. When this anger is forcibly suppressed or for other reasons insufficiently expressed, it may fester within and create a cumulative effect with time.

But even this forcible suppression is more likely to result in psychosomatic illnesses (headaches, ulcers, heart problems), than in violent behavior in the average person. Most people occasionally experience a fleeting flush of anger that might result in throwing something across the room, kicking a chair, or screaming obscenities, but not, except in fantasy, result in a direct act of violence against a person. In fact, many therapy groups encourage the verbal release of pent-up anger as a way of releasing tension and reaffirming self-esteem.

Negative, hostile, and violent feelings almost always emerge in the treatment of adolescents, and often these feelings represent a way of relating and indicating that a bond exists. In children and adolescents the ability to verbalize feelings is an important alternative to acting them out through violent behavior.

The Biological Roots of Anger

Anger springs from the deepest and most primitive part of the brain. Electrodes placed against the hypothalamus of cats can induce instant rage at the flip of a switch. The cerebral cortex, the reasoning part of the brain, covers and controls these inner primitive centers. Walter Cannon, the famous physiologist from Harvard University, was intrigued by his discovery in the 1930's that the removal of the cerebral hemispheres resulted in an extraordinary exhibition of rage. Similarly, anything that disturbs the regulatory function of the cerebral cortex, i.e., brain damage, drugs, alcohol, malnutrition, and chronic stress, can result in increased irritability, intolerance to stress, frustration, and in predisposed individuals, to acts of violence.

Anger blocks thinking and creativity, constricts the flow of blood to the internal organs, holds the heart in a tight grip, and literally blinds us to the potential for loving communication with others. When a person is in a state of extreme rage, his body is flushed with adrenaline and the rational part of the brain is partially paralyzed. All behavior is momentarily under the control of instinctive survival reactions, or learned responses from earlier experiences, and the modeling provided by adults who expressed rage during that person's childhood.

Rage reactions such as temper tantrums, throwing

the hammer with which you accidentally hit your finger, screaming, complaining over a traffic citation, and threatening the dog next door for knocking down your garbage cans cannot be included in the category of violence. These behaviors represent episodes of momentary outlets for frustration (emotional release), rather than total loss of emotional control.

One of the most uncomfortable revelations that patients discover during the course of personal analysis is their volcano of inner rage that has its roots in childhood, and which has been covered over with polite behavior.

Where does all this anger come from? Karl Menninger believed that the human infant begins his life in anger. Even the most attentive mother may arouse a rage reaction in her baby when she doesn't respond immediately to the child's cries of hunger. Later, that child may hate the newborn baby sister for diverting mother's attention from him. However, unless anger is sanctioned in the environment, it quickly goes underground in order to buy love.

Fritz Redl, author of the book, *Children Who Hate,* claims that the hate mass is formed during a baby's first two years, and that its size depends upon the amount of genuine affection the baby receives and how much independence the child is permitted. Emotional impoverishment results in a flood of fury at the slightest frustration, which a healthy child might quickly check by shifting toward an enjoyable substitute activity.

However, children who have no happy memories to fall back upon will seek a target to attack to modulate their tension. But even here, the expression of anger will be based upon what they learned directly or indirectly from their parents, in the parents' own handling of anger.

Anger always justifies itself. Reality becomes distorted as emotion skews perceptions. Arguments only add fuel to the fire, both parties saying to themselves: "Again, I'm not understood." "Again, I'm always the one who's wrong." "Again, no one cares how I feel." Because of our ingrained patterns of response, and the power of the emotions associated with these patterns, we can, at best, have only limited and temporary control over our behavior unless we change the underlying attitudes that prompt the behavioral responses. These attitudes toward ourselves and the world we live in come both from our parents and from our educational system.

Anger is always a call for help, an expression of a defeat, of not being able to use more creative ways to maintain one's integrity. An example might be seen in children teasing each other. The one who fails to come up with a clever retort becomes enraged.

Hate, regardless of how it is demonstrated, is usually the outgrowth of self-hate. The less emotionally mature the individual, the more he hates, and the more he will obsess over sadistic fantasies for revenge. While such an individual may never actually become violent, he will inevitably become self-destructive in his close relationships.

Genetic Predisposition to Violent Behavior

The discussion of violent behavior would be incomplete without addressing the issue of temperament. A growing number of psychiatrists believe that there is a biochemical or genetic predisposition to violent behavior. There is no denying the link of testosterone to aggressive behavior. Boys are significantly more aggressive than girls in their play. Males are responsible for up to 90% of all violent crimes. More recently, a number of studies have indicated an abnormally low level of serotonin in the blood of men predisposed to criminality. Serotonin is a hormone implicated in affective or mood disorders. The amino acid, tryptophan, is a precursor of serotonin and is found in most foods. Some recent studies have suggested that there is a lowering of blood serotonin in people who are eating low cholesterol diets, and that this increases their level of chronic irritability and hostility.

Chromosome abnormalities have recently been detected in individuals predisposed to criminality, as have genetic traits toward poor impulse control. These traits can be detected by the third grade. Such children compulsively engage in aggressive, disruptive behavior regardless of consequences, as if they have little or no self-control. Many fit the diagnostic category of Attention Deficit Disorder with Conduct Disturbance.

Drs. Ervin and Mark at Massachusetts General Hospital in Boston described some 25 years ago the Dyscontrol Syndrome in men who often had abnormal brain waves. These men, probably a small but significant percentage of our male population, can be triggered into rage at the slightest provocation.

In a typical incident, one man went out of control with rage when someone pulled in front of his car on the freeway. He chased the car for two miles, honking wildly, and finally forced it off the road. He then got out, smashed the front door window, and was wrestling with the driver when police intervened.

From birth all humans exhibit individual differences in their reactivity to the environment. At least a dozen different personality characteristics can readily be observed even in newborns in the nursery. These include sensitivity, the need for cuddling, irritability, crying, general motor activity, etc.

Behavior in all living organisms is the outcome of the environment acting upon genetic potential. Out of this fact has come the nature-versus-nurture debate as to which has predominant importance. *The higher the organism is upon the evolutionary chain, measured by the development of the brain and the neurological system, the more significant are the environmental factors that shape behavior.*

I have found that a good environment can modify or override the behavioral problems of many hyper-aggressive children. This finding also appears to be borne out in research with rhesus monkeys. Steven Suomi, head of research of a rhesus monkey colony run by the National Institute of Child Health and Development, reported that the most aggressive monkeys had the lowest level of blood serotonin, genetically. However, what mattered most in determining personality was the environment and the kind of mothering the monkey received. Young monkeys, born with low serotonin, put into peer groups with an artificial mother that supplied only milk, were most likely to display violent behavior as adult monkeys. However, those placed with nurturing mothers grew up to be more normal.

Harry Harlow, experimenting on caged rhesus monkeys in the 1960's at the University of Wisconsin, showed that babies deprived of a mother grew up to be severely warped in personality, unable to fit into monkey society, and were prone to random acts of violence. However, he also showed that deprived and behaviorally impaired monkeys could be rescued by exposing them to younger, normal monkeys for as little as an hour a day. The same approach has been applied successfully in treating emotionally withdrawn human children.

Chapter Three

Bonding and
Role Confusion

Most of my professional life has been devoted to teaching parents, teachers, and correctional officers how to discipline the infant child, the adolescent, or the young adult under their tutelage and care. My major task is always directly related to the problem of the unawareness and insensitivity of the person in authority as to the effects their own behavior has upon the mental state of their charge. I have found that making analogies to dog training can be very useful in bringing objective understanding to the true nature of the relationship.

For example, parents will complain that despite the fact that they are very firm, clear and directive with their young son, he still pouts or stubbornly resists obeying their wishes. I have them describe a specific incident and then ask: Suppose that you were invited to the home of a professional dog trainer who owned a pet German Shepherd. During the course of the evening, you hear the dog barking at a cat in the backyard, which disturbs your conversation. Your friend shouts, "Rex." No response. With an angrier tone, he yells, "Rex," again. Finally, he gets up and drags the dog by the collar into the room, pushes him down beside his chair and gives his rump a sharp whack. The dog lets out a "yipe" and then remains frozen in his position. Would you be impressed with this performance? Definitely not, if you had ever witnessed the interaction between a properly disciplined German Shepherd and his master. You would never see a need for reprimand or slapping.

Yet, in a similar situation, if the young son were playing too noisily in the other room, and he ignored a shout to "quiet down," you might be impressed with the parent who bodily yanks the child into the room, pats his fanny and firmly sits him down on a chair, where he remains quietly. I ask: What do you think is going on in the head of that child? And what kind of relationship is being established between the father and the child? Everything evolves around relationship.

This example is given because it appears to be a mild, "so-what" situation. But the child most likely experiences humiliation and deep-seated resentment because of a lack of sensitivity and respect for the special bond he thinks he had with his father. Would a respected adult friend be treated this way? In every encounter, always consider the effect of your behavior upon the long-term nature of the relationship. All future interaction is predicated upon this.

The need to bond with a strong, stable authority figure begins with the family unit. Because human behavior is more dependent upon learning than is the behavior of lower animals, socialization of the child is primarily effected by identification with his parents, and the development of conscience reflects the parents' conscience, as well.

Trust and respect for authority figures also begins in the home, first from the child's attitude toward the parents and secondarily, from the parents' attitudes toward teachers, religious leaders, and political figures in the greater community. The more consistent and warm the parents are toward the child, and the less authoritative or over-indulgent they are, the better the child's relationships with his peers.

Every child seeks to find a sense of significance by pleasing his or her parents by being like them. Little boys and girls who try to help their fathers and mothers with household chores or gardening are devastated when they are criticized for "doing it wrong," or "being clumsy," instead of being praised for their desire to form a loving partnership. Their attempt to find acceptance by pleasing their parent has backfired.

Arguments between the two parents, provided there is some caring and an eventual resolution, can be a valuable learning experience for the child. However, altercations in which one parent belittles or verbally or physically abuses the other, creates considerable inner conflict inasmuch as the child identifies with both parents. Also, it is difficult for a child to receive love from a degraded parent without hating the other parent. A single-parent family in this case is far preferable, especially if there are visitation rights which allow the child to establish an independent bond with each parent.

A distinct generation boundary between a parent and child is essential to maintaining a mutual bond of respect and trust. However, sometimes one parent will turn to the child for support against the other parent for reassurance, or to fill an emotional need. An extreme example of this is sexual molestation, which has devastating emotional consequences for the child.

A relatively more common breach of the "generation boundary" rule occurs when a guilty or needy parent with low self-esteem tries to buy love from a child by assuming a submissive, servitude pattern by constant catering to the child's every whim, thus forcing a dominance pattern upon the child. The child may become "spoiled," demanding, or confused regarding what to feel toward the parent. Behind this is a feeling of being manipulated or controlled.

This servitude pattern in a mother can have an emotionally crippling effect upon a child. The child may grow into an emotionally immature and self-centered adult, dependent upon the mother and tending to marry late in life, if at all. Or the child, in a desperate attempt to gain autonomy, may try to maintain as much distance from the mother as possible, while dutifully keeping a mechanical and polite relationship by telephone, preferably long-distance. Somewhat tongue-in-cheek, I have suggested to my psychology students that the West Coast was populated by young adults fleeing from smothering East Coast mothers with low self-esteem, who gave love for the purpose of receiving love.

The need to gain acceptance and love by giving acceptance and love makes women, as a group, especially vulnerable to enabling behavior or co-dependent behavior. *Men find a sense of significance through doing, impressing, and being a hero. Women find a sense of significance in giving nurturance* and in giving of themselves freely to a man who resonates emotional pain similar to their own, and who appears to be starving for affection and love.

However, in enabling a needy man she perpetuates his sense of helplessness and immaturity and, eventually, he will become abusive in order to regain his autonomy and re-establish the masculine-dominant role. This is a common syndrome experienced by women who "Love Too Much."

Chapter Four

Power Struggles

All of us have experienced being on one side or another of a power struggle at some time in our life. In fact, some people believe that power struggles are an unavoidable part of every relationship. Who's calling the shots? If they are trying to do it without agreement, then there's going to be a hassle. Even when there is a designated authority figure such as parent, teacher or supervisor, the ongoing struggle to maintain power and control against covert and overt opposition seems interminable. I have been called in as a consultant many times in all of these situations.

Parents come to me complaining: "I can't get him to obey, no matter how hard we punish him." Teachers complain, "I don't have time to analyze his family background, I just want this student to stop disrupting the class." Executive officers of large corporations want to know, "How can I improve morale? How can I get these people to follow orders without dragging their feet?"

Power struggles evolve around the issue of control. *They result from a lack of clear-cut delineation of roles, or a lack of respect for the designated authority figure.* Power struggles manifest in a number of ways, from overt rebellion against all control to more subtle expressions of defiance, including harassment and partial compliance, designed to frustrate the authority figure.

Most power struggles are learned behavior. Children, for example, learn to capitalize on the weaknesses of their parents to resist their control. They quickly sense the parents' guilt, self-doubt, lack of clarity, and need for acceptance by the child. This allows them to get away with slow, impartial compliance or even total disregard for rules. These energy-draining power struggles can make a nightmare out of parenting and teaching the young, and yet they are totally self-created by the person in authority.

A power struggle may be defined as a battle of wills between a subordinate and a person in a designated position of authority. In the usual case, the authority figure attempts to maintain the power position by utilizing considerable energy in the form of force, threat, bribery or punishment to enforce compliance. Resistance against this energy may take on many forms and may range from subtle and covert to outright rebellion. Authority figures expect their wishes to be carried out either through willing compliance or by enforced control. Willing compliance is attainable only in an atmosphere of mutual respect and trust between an authority figure and a subordinate. When this trust is lacking, a power struggle will eventually arise out of the issue of control.

Parents are notorious for inflicting their wills upon their infant children in a controlling manner that arouses anger and resistance. Anger is the natural biological response to enforced helplessness, fear, humiliation, or a felt attack upon self-concept.

For example, any sudden disruption of the natural flow of an ongoing activity, whether it be motoric play, exploratory curiosity, or pleasurable exercising of the five senses, results in a blockage of energy that leaves a sense of incompleteness, and evokes an inner protest. The more frequently that barriers to natural expression are imposed, the greater the build-up of frustration, especially in the absence of clearly defined acceptable activity. Thus, a series of insensitive No's, imposed midstream on an already initiated activity by an intolerant parent, can push almost any child into a temper tantrum. This is an example of overt control by the parent in which compliance is attained by intimidation or physical force. Note that willing compliance might easily be attained if the parent became sensitively involved in the activity, and then redirected it into a more acceptable area without damming up the energy.

As the child grows older, shaming and guilt are common means of controlling the initiation of unwanted behavior. The fear of upsetting a brittle parent, and then being made to feel totally unworthy of love, is a major deterrent to the spontaneous expression of any emotion or activity. Children have an innate need to please and to gain acceptance. Any behavior that brings a response of praise or an expression of love will compulsively be repeated over and over again. Even adults, like children, also get a sense of personal power and self-satisfaction which is dependent upon their ability to please or to impress others.

There is no one more important to a child, no one whose praise is more valued, than a parent. Every parent has all of the advantages over their child that they could possibly need to guarantee blind obedience, namely awe, respect, dependency, a need for love and a desire for praise. Yet, sadly, all too soon, parents lose both respect and trust by needlessly attempting to enforce obedience through reprimand, coercion, punishment and guilt.

When a parent is impossible to please, the child feels powerless, and may give up trying to earn love. Once a child feels that he is unloved and that his own personal needs are not a high priority, his willingness to obey the wishes of a parent markedly diminishes. This only reinforces the parents' attempts to control by breaking the will, and thus seeking subservient behavior rather than willing behavior.

Every child during the early years, from about age two to six, attempts to establish a devotional bond with both parents. These attempts are usually extinguished by a father's indifference, or discouraged by a mother's refusal to be pleased. Yet the need is so strong that children will persist through the latency years to buy love, despite all types of discouragement or abuse. Parents, instead of reinforcing the will to serve, often try to enforce subservient behavior through threats or physical abuse. These attempts result in power struggles against doing homework, emptying the garbage, or mowing the lawn.

Whenever there is a strong disagreement or resentment against the prevailing authority, and especially one that has the power to make decisions which critically impact our survival, be it parent, boss, or political leader, we invariably will experience a sense of insecurity and inner conflict. There may even be some fear of reprisal should our disagreements become exposed, and thus putting us in an open adversarial position in which we are the definite underdog. There is a rebellious streak in most of us, usually kept underground for the sake of maintaining peace. Most children, for example, will acknowledge being relieved that the adults about them cannot "read their minds."

Inner resentment and feelings of "it isn't fair," are often suppressed until the teen years when independence is less frightening, and when peer support is available. Some rebellion at this age is necessary and healthy for individuation and need not be of so much concern to parents who are sometimes shocked by the dramatic changes their "good" little boy or girl may go through between the ages of 12 and 16.

Reprimand and punishment only alienate the child from the parents. Such responses instill a negative self-concept that is no longer capable of earning love. Control of behavior through coercion and guilt arouses inner rebellion and defiance. A vicious cycle occurs in which the angry, hurt, and humiliated child engages in a variety of power struggles with the frustrated and emotionally drained parent who intensifies attempts to break the will of the child through increased punishment and threats.

The pattern of power struggles learned in the home is carried over into the greater community. *Thus, the integrity of the family unit becomes the core strength of any great society.* Power struggles represent a breakdown in discipline which results from a lack of respect for the person in the authority position. Punishment, then, becomes necessary to maintain control. The need for excessive physical force or violence to maintain civil control always signals the beginning of the end of the regime in power. The polarities have widened beyond repair, and a pattern of defiance is now clearly established.

The Vietnam War is a case in point. Prior to this period it was almost unthinkable to resist the draft or to oppose a war. But here there began a gradual distrust of the motives of our national leaders, and of the manner in which the war was conducted. Once protests began, primarily by students on college campuses, they spread rapidly. The use of violence at Kent State marked the beginning of the end of broad public support for the war. This power struggle arose from an attempt by the ruling authority to maintain control by suppressing the free expression of criticism. Paradoxically, the opportunity to speak out lessens the likelihood of rebellion.

Similarly, an experienced parent is able to handle a toddler's assertive "No" in a benign, non-suppressive fashion. By acknowledging the feelings of the child, a parent conveys the sense of significance the child is seeking, and this action quickly dissipates the child's motivation for defiance.

There are a few important prerequisites for attaining compliant behavior. Any individual's behavior is highly dependent upon the structure of the setting and the quality of the authority figure in charge. An environment that is properly structured to encourage compliant behavior, whether it be the home, a classroom, an office, or a prison setting, must provide positive answers to the three basic survival questions in order to minimize power struggles.

Survival Questions

(1) **WHO AM I?** Is the individual able to identify with the person in authority in terms of respecting the

authority figure's goals and responsibilities, while simultaneously feeling valued personally as someone whose basic needs and rights as a human being are respected?

(2) **AM I SAFE?** Is the society or person in authority sufficiently strong and willing to be responsible for ensuring my safety from physical abuse, harassment, and victimization by anyone else sharing the environment? Will personal boundaries be respected? Will reasonable accommodations be provided for food, water, clothing, and other basic survival needs?

(3) **CAN I COPE?** Will the expectations upon me be reasonable and consistent and will opportunities be available to maintain a sense of significance by being allowed some form of personal expression and recognition?

No person or group can function optimally in any setting until these three questions are appropriately resolved. And each setting has its own set of answers. Thus, a child who has problems at home may be a model student in school, and conversely, a disruptive student may be a leader on the basketball court. This means that every authority figure, given the proper support system, must be personally responsible for the behavior of those placed in his charge.

A true leader has the respect, trust, and devotion of followers, which enables him to lead them through sacrifices and deprivation without resistance. On the other hand, most dictators maintain control through fear, intimidation, punishment and oppression. The energy of constant vigilance needed to enforce compliance under those conditions will ultimately drain the resources of his country.

At the other extreme is the weak leader or the insecure parent who uses catering to be accepted and liked, and bribery to buy cooperation. This creates a major shift in the motivational energy of the child or a subordinate from one of seeking praise to one of feeling manipulated. The pattern of catering and bribery becomes an expectation, and then soon becomes a demand, and the price keeps getting higher. No one is more disliked than a leader who is afraid of his responsibility. A strong leader may not be liked, but might still be respected, and his orders followed without question, provided they serve a common good.

If the fear of punishment is the only incentive for compliant behavior, eventually a tolerance breakdown may occur in which the consequences have lost their meaning. This can lead, on a family level, to a battered wife shooting her husband, and on a national level to revolution or anarchy.

Anarchy, a state of total social upheaval, occurs only in the absence of a respected leader or a loss of faith in the political system. The fear of mob rule, which inevitably fosters uncontrolled violence, has led past populations of republics and democracies to elect, out of desperation, a dictatorship in an attempt to maintain order through unrestrained power. This is the challenge that faces the new democracies of the former U.S.S.R. today.

Chapter Five

Crazymaking

If we observe animals in their natural habitat, we see that they are usually relaxed and content. So, too, we might conjecture that the natural state of humans is to be happy, loving, creative, and content. Civilizations evolved with the purpose of creating an environment wherein this natural state would be made possible for larger numbers of people. Yet, the mental state that we encounter in others and experience in ourselves is commonly quite the opposite.

Somehow, we all seem to understand what a person who says, "I feel crazy," means. How do different people describe the experience? Craziness is a state of upset, overwhelm, and turmoil in the head, with no known solution. It is often associated with physical exhaustion, headache, emotional depression or apprehension. The first thing a husband may hear when he comes home is, "The kids are driving me crazy!" And if the kids had a voice they would probably retort, "Mommy is driving us crazy!"

Exhaustion can result from overwork without proper rest. However, strenuous activity, when it is exciting, may leave one feeling "tired," but certainly not feeling "crazy," which the old family doctors called "having a nervous breakdown."

The cause of feeling crazy is stress, and stress is caused by inner conflict, when the mind is filled with unresolved input that creates tension and anxiety. Stress occurs when the innate instincts and the learned, social instincts are at war with each other. There exists a paralysis resulting from inner rebellion, guilt, helplessness, and self-doubt. This is one definition of neurosis, and hardly anyone is free from it.

The pattern for neurosis begins in childhood. Young children have the extraordinary talent of attuning their minds to the consciousness of the adults about them. If their parents' heads are filled with fear, anger, and worry, the growing brain of the child will attune to this, independent of the parents' words and actions. Thus, children adopt from parental figures a pattern of moods and feelings that can last a lifetime, and which they transmit to their own children.

Equally important, each child is born with innate social drives that need reinforcement and positive feedback if they are not to be extinguished. For example, Harlow's experiments with monkeys and Bowlby's experiments with dogs raised in an environment without a nurturing mother and without physical petting showed that the young developed an irritable temperament and antisocial behaviors.

Thus, children who are not hugged grow into adults who do not like to be touched. During the first five years of life, the developing brain is dependent upon environmental input. Sensory organs, when unused, may never develop. For example, cats raised in the dark become blind, and children not exposed to speech until the age of six rarely learn to talk.

The majority of our children today are raised in abnormal environments. If not directly the target of parental anger and frustration, they are even more crippled by sins of omission. A child needs focused attention, physical embracing, and a loving atmosphere. Books written on self-esteem emphasize the importance of feeling loved in early childhood.

Over the years I have come to realize that even more important than being loved is having someone who appreciates your love. You empower others by how you receive what they have to give. How often do you see little children with their hearts wide open, reaching out to give love to a mommy and daddy who shove them aside, or tell them to stop being a nuisance? The need for a love bond to mommy and daddy is so strong that children, like puppy dogs, persist for years to form such a bond, despite repeated rejection. They are made to feel guilty for being needy. And even more devastating, the love they have to give is seen as having no value.

What makes a child feel "crazy"? When his head is filled with input that doesn't meld together, and nothing he does is right. Add guilt, suppress his emotions, and surround the child with intolerant adults who are so filled with anxiety and fear that they don't notice their effect upon him, and you pretty much have the usual case of what it's like to be a child in our society, today.

We can make mice neurotic (or crazy) in the laboratory setting by giving them the kind of inconsistent feedback that most children experience every day. For example, we can place mice in a metal cage with a white line on the floor dividing the cage in two. When we want the mice to cross the line, we administer a mild shock to the metal plate on the side where the mice are placed. The mice learn quickly to leap to safety over the white line to the other half of the cage.

As long as this pattern is consistent, the mice appear to be minimally disturbed by the inconvenience.

However, start administering the shocks randomly and inconsistently, and the mice will soon huddle helplessly in a corner, gradually ignoring the shocks. Their behavior will remain distinctly abnormal and remain erratic for some time after all shocking has ceased.

You can understand that screaming at a child for behavior over which he has minimal control can be devastating to his self-image. Also chastising a child for a behavior he learned indirectly through your modeling, or inconsistently expanding and contracting his limits, is "crazy-making." Thus, it is necessary that you, as an adult, must be responsible for and in control of your own behavior at all times. Otherwise you will become emotionally reactive to unwanted behavior, thus giving up your power to the child and to consequently reducing yourself to coping with the situation at the child's level.

Let us compare the average infant child's situation to a comparable situation with an animal such as a dog. The mother dog rests peacefully until a stranger approaches. Then the mother dog may bark or snarl until the stranger leaves, and when she resumes her peaceful posture. This is all quite understandable to her puppy, who has no need to deny or repress reality or to suppress its own emotional reactions to this scenario.

In the case of a human infant, however, there is no

such thing as mother assuming a restful state of peace, nor is there usually any visible scenario to explain the "craziness" in mother's head, to which the child is attuned. Moreover, the child is at high risk of becoming, unpredictably, a verbal or physical target of a highly stressed mother, with shattering consequences to the child's delicate nervous system.

In addition, a child will take each such attack, reprimand, or sense of rejection personally, with devastating repercussions for his or her self-concept. Physically the body becomes armored, the muscles become tense, especially the jaw, throat, chest, shoulders, and pelvis, in an attempt to numb all sensation. But again, unlike the puppy dog, a child has no "safe" time in which to release his guard.

Children cannot gain a sense of significance from parents who, themselves, have no strong sense of significance. Crazymaking in the home occurs when a child is reprimanded for innate behaviors, such as shouting, running, curiosity-seeking, and attempting to gain mastery over the physical environment, especially when positive options are lacking. The parents may be depressed or angry and impossible for the child to please. Guilt, physical abuse, and neglect become introjected into the child's self-image.

The home environment of most children is periodically filled with anxiety and fear, while unreasonable and inconsistent expectations for compliance are placed upon them. Additionally, an emotionally depressed woman, even though she may mother with good intentions, is mistaken in thinking that she is giving love. The presence of a depressed mother infuses the child with depressive feelings, and in the absence of a strong male presence makes children irritable, restless, and apprehensive.

The lack, in most homes, of a strong and supportive male presence to provide a stabilizing influence is resulting in a growing population of teenagers who feel no connection to each other or to the established order. In boys this can lead to the need for affiliation with a gang for a sense of identity, as well as for security. Also, the easy availability of guns provides them with the ultimate security blanket. Thus, crazymaking in the home forces the emancipated teenagers to seek an escape from their inner chaos and confusion through alcohol, drugs, and sexual promiscuity, or to find some form of identity through the joining of cults or gangs.

The Growth of Street Gangs

The increasing numbers of street gangs in our inner cities is a symptom of the growing alienation between a significant segment of our young people today, and the social structure. While working in the California Youth Authority I observed that teenage criminals who were about to be released back into society often behaved as if their impending freedom was burdensome, or even dangerous. They were leaving a setting that was safe, predictable, and relatively free from conflict, to re-enter a street environment where survival is a predominant concern, where there is a sense of alienation from the greater society, and where they have little opportunity to experience significance or purpose.

A lack of respect and trust in the prevailing authority structure is usually accompanied by fear and dread.

However, in the extremely stressful and abnormal subculture of street-gang existence, fear no longer serves as a useful ally. Fear, like all powerful emotions, is highly contagious and must be repressed. In its place is seen the cold, callous, unemotional façade of one who has already accepted his death. Those who cannot repress their fear become targets of attack, as if they carry a virus that must not be allowed to spread.

The alienation that they feel from the outer world, in which they have no real place or role, and the void within their male identity, resulting from an absent father, is resolved by identification with a small, similarly afflicted subculture. They see this alternative as a voluntary option that gives them a sense of freedom of choice. The seductive aspect is the illusion of choice, that "my fate depends upon me, on my words, on my attitude." In reality it involves progressive compliance with the gang's values in order to minimize emotional conflict and to gain acceptance. By adopting the gang and "choosing" to interject it as one's own world, a sense of intactness is maintained.

The abolition of fear is accompanied by a closing of the heart. There is a lack of empathy for the suffering of others, with often, a paradoxical sentimentality. A teenage gang member may cry at the sound of familiar music or at the death of a puppy. On the other hand, a victim pleading for mercy may activate memories of his own earlier feelings of helplessness, which he then seeks to obliterate through inflicting increased sadism upon his victim.

Chapter Six

The Pecking Order

The pecking order, first noted in bumblebees, means that A pecks B, B pecks C, etc. Some form of pecking order has been noted in most social structures, including those of birds, fish, and even insects, in addition to mammals. The existence of a pecking order does not mean that the dominant male assumes any particular leadership responsibility within the hierarchy. In fact, such a phenomenon is not always associated directly with social behaviors.

Dominance behavior is sometimes evidenced as antisocial behavior, probably prompted by the instinct for self-preservation in overcrowded, competitive environments. Overcrowding leads to many social abnormalities in animals. Crowded rats, for example, display increased fights, hypersexuality, and cannibalism. Crowding almost any two solitary animals together will produce a dominance hierarchy in which one animal becomes boss or kills the other. This is the major cause of death in zoos and aquariums.

This truth is an interesting thought to ponder in view of the importance that hierarchal systems play in human interaction. Well-defined and modulated hierarchal systems may provide a stabilizing factor to the social order. However, all too often the social desire for personal dominance results in aggressive behavior to establish a higher position in an ever-shifting pecking order.

The major theme of some of the most popular TV soap operas in the past decade, such as "Dallas," "Dynasty," and "Falcon Crest," involves the continual battling for dominance among affluent and powerful men and women who otherwise appear to have everything the material world has to offer.

In contrast, the dominance hierarchy in social animals, such as baboons, wolves, and birds, is relatively stable from day to day. Conflicts are rare, because one animal will usually step aside to one of higher rank. Interestingly, a female baboon, when mated to a higher ranking baboon, assumes a higher rank. This is one avenue in our own society by which women may also attempt to rise in the pecking order.

Within the animal kingdom there also exist innate patterns of submissiveness that have the effect of diminishing the aggressive drive of a dominant animal. For example, one pack wolf might offer its throat to a stronger wolf to ward off an attack. This behavior is akin to the advice of "turning the other cheek," purportedly to drain the wrath of an adversary and to check the escalation of hostilities.

The overall purpose of a pecking order and of submissive behavior patterns in social animals may be to minimize fighting by establishing a firm, unchallenged hierarchial structure, thus diminishing the provocation of aggressive behavior.

Every stable social structure is maintained by some form of hierarchical system that places each member in a fairly defined place in the pecking order. The more clearly defined the levels and the more available the opportunities to improve one's status within the order, the more stable is the structure, i.e., there are fewer conflicts and power struggles and thus a reduced need for policing behavior.

A good example of this stability is the military establishment. Each rank has specific responsibilities as well as privileges. There is some opportunity to rise within the system, and an equal guarantee of personal rights, which insures a sense of significance at every level. Provisions exist for health care, food, and shelter, which makes the military an enticing career path for many, despite the drawback of low financial remuneration. Japanese corporations have operated from a somewhat similar model with much success. However, such a model may also discourage creativity and individuality.

A social system in which there is an almost perfect distribution of labor for the common good exists in the sponge. A sponge is essentially a large colony of single celled organisms, called protozoans. Some cells can hold on in swift currents, while some can secrete skeletons and others concentrate on food-getting. This model symbolizes something like the social system that the founders of communism initially envisioned, i.e., an equal division of labor for the common good.

But its application to the human condition has obvious pitfalls, not the least of which is that sponges have not evolved significantly over millions of years. Sometimes a society that takes responsibility for filling all of our needs can be just as debilitating to our will as one that is indifferent or suppressive of our needs.

On the other hand, a democratic society may engender insecurity because each person is largely responsible for his own survival needs. And, despite constitutional safeguards, equal opportunity for security and comfort is not provided for all, and competition leads to stress, which shortens the lives of even the most successful executives of large corporations.

A typical social hierarchy for almost any political structure might be delineated as follows:

> King, President, Dictator
> Top influential leaders
> Privileged class
> General population
> Underprivileged class

These strata of relative levels of influence, wealth, and power are difficult to eliminate in practice, even in *The Republic* of Plato or in the socialism of Karl Marx. It is the nature of people to put relative status upon certain abilities or attributes, whether these traits are earned or gifted from birth. In this country, various surveys have indicated that the status ladder is something like the following:

> White
> Male
> Protestant
> Wealthy family
> Highly educated
> Executive Officer of large corporation
> High political position or influence

Special achievement: fame in sports, entertainment, or writing

At the bottom level of the structure we might include:

The homeless
The mentally unfit
Welfare recipients
Prison population
The educationally illiterate
Unwed mothers
Delinquent teenagers

The mistake that most ruling classes appear to have made, historically, which eventually contributed to the crumbling of the entire structure around them, was to ignore their responsibility to the lower strata. Eventually a tolerance breakdown occurs and pockets of unrest erupt. When this unrest is put down with force, rather than by addressing the real problems, it simmers beneath the surface, until it gains the power for a full-blown revolution.

As long as we are dealing with human nature there is no social structure that can work perfectly. However, almost every social system works best when all of its citizenry are united against a common enemy in times of war. The real challenge comes after the outer enemy has been vanquished and the borders are secure. Then the call for patriotism loses its voice.

Now the focus shifts to an inner maneuvering of relative power and status within the various strata of the hierarchy. And the greater the population density, the greater the incidents of conflict. An external enemy is never as deadly as the enemy within.

Konrad Lorenz observes in his classic book, *On Aggression*, that the greatest danger to every species does not come from the natural enemies of that species, but rather from those who share the same eating chain. Thus, civil wars have a tendency to be the most bloody, and rioting mobs characteristically seek targets within their own neighborhoods.

Dominant Behavior and the Pecking Order

In social animals, dominance is established by a variety of visual or behavioral cues that do not involve the brutalization of other pack members. Only in special situations where dominance is challenged does it involve a physical contest. And, once dominance is established, there is rarely a second challenge. Establishing dominance, especially in humans, is not directly related to establishing responsibility or respect within the social system.

For example, a bully in the school yard may establish dominance by his threatening demeanor, but will not necessarily obtain obedience, and certainly not loyalty. Obedience is dependent upon establishing a devotional bond based on mutual trust and respect. *Dominance based upon intimidation may secure momentary subservient compliance, but eventually anger will overcome fear, and rebellion or violence may result.*

Dominant behavior in men and women can be measured by the willingness of each to challenge directly the views, opinions, or status of another person. Women do not differ from men in this respect when they are part of the same peer group, such as the same class in college.

Dominant behavior has to do primarily with affirming one's own position, and is only indirectly related to aggressive behavior that involves the active attempt to influence or to control another for personal gain.

Whenever you question, challenge, or refuse to accept the advice of another person, you threaten their claim to a dominant status. Children who do this to adults are considered rude. "They don't know their place." Young girls are especially sensitive to comments made about them, such as: "Who does she think she is?" Teenagers coming into their own power get into arguments with their parents, who refuse to give up dominance.

Arguments by married couples have little to do with the subject of the argument, and everything to do with trying to affirm a higher status than the other person is giving to them. Most commonly, this is done in a defensive manner by invalidating the ideas or motives of the other person.

Deplorably, this mutually destructive pattern has been adopted by political candidates who try to persuade the electorate of their own superiority by degrading their opponent. This practice succeeds only in devaluing both parties and winning votes for "None of the Above." Likewise, sexual harassment in the workplace is more often a matter of establishing gender dominance than of sexuality, per se.

When one's dominance is clearly and comfortably established within a given social structure, there is very little stress associated with holding the dominant position. However, trying to maintain the dominant position in an unstable hierarchy is highly stressful, and a risk factor for heart disease in young executives.

Dominance is related to relative status within a particular group. It differs from setting to setting, depending upon talents and ties of friendship. Talk show host Johnny Carson acknowledged that he is relatively shy, socially, in contrast to his dominant behavior on the "Tonight Show," where, according to his own words, he "has total control."

There is a natural tendency, as one grows older, to be drawn more and more to environments that raise one's dominance status and to avoid those which do not. Thus, a successful physician or businessman who does not know how to be a husband or father will find excuses to work long hours, which keeps him away from the family. Workalcoholics are those who are compulsively driven to engage in some activity that brings them a sense of accomplishment, while avoiding their true responsibilities within the context of their family circle.

Women, regardless of race, have been placed in a relatively minor place in the pecking order in most societies in the world. Even Switzerland, one of the most progressive of democratic nations, did not allow women to vote until 1971.

What this means, in a real sense, is that women have had to learn submissive patterns to minimize the escalation of male dominant patterns against them. Most girls learn, before puberty, to adopt "neutralizing" patterns against sexually aggressive overtures. This includes looking away, focusing intently upon something else, maintaining a bland expression, and assuming a hunched, asexual posture.

However, almost nothing will work if the girl inadvertently initiated the interest by a long stare, for example. Then the boy will wait patiently for a glance back or a quivering of the lips that will mean to him that a coy, courting game is going on. This can lead to sexual harassment of one type or another, including date rape, and women, until recently, have tended to blame themselves for it.

Every psychologist who works with child molestation and incest must learn to deal with the guilt and shame of the young victim who feels compelled to maintain her secret because of a fear of blame. Somehow, the myth of an inability of the average male to control his sexual impulses has persisted over the centuries and excused men from taking full responsibility for their sexual proclivities.

The media contributes heavily to the linking of masculinity and charisma with sexual promiscuity. Sexual prowess is a curious human preoccupation unknown in any other living species. It is one instinct over which men are not sufficiently encouraged, by society, to exercise a disciplined mind. Increasingly, rape and other forms of sexual and physical aggression against women are becoming a way in which inadequate men feel free to exercise dominant predatory behaviors seen only in wild animals raised in unnatural environments.

What is particularly ominous for the survival of the human race is the current distortion of what Konrad Lorenz calls "Moral Instincts," or special inhibitions against aggression, which he observed in social animals.

An animal mother is prevented by special inhibitions from aggressiveness toward her own children. The turkey hen, for example, is prevented from attacking her brood by an inhibition elicited by their chirping. So, too, infant children have endearing smiles, chortling, and other instinctive patterns to elicit a mothering response. Dogs have an inhibitory mechanism that prevents them from seriously attacking puppies under the age of seven to eight months.

An equally important observation made by Lorenz is that, "In animals there is a whole series of species in which, under normal, that is, non-pathological conditions, a male never seriously attacks a female." He adds, "This is true of our domestic dog and doubtless of the wolf too. I would not trust a dog that bit bitches, and would warn his owner to be most careful, especially if there were children in the house."

Women and Family Violence

Battered, abused, and abandoned women constitute the major problem facing our country today. All of the other ills of society stem from this origin because of the deleterious effect of stressed and depressed mothers upon their children. We must not ignore the research that clearly shows that animals raised by mothers in a state of fear or depression grow into asocial, irritable, and fearful adults with poor control over impulses. This situation of the dehumanizing treatment of women is finally beginning to be recognized openly, but is not likely to change dramatically until respect for women is instilled at all levels: the family, the church, the schools, and the workplace.

The increase in incidents of male violence upon women is an ominous indicator of the progressive mental dysfunction of our male population created by an insensitive educational system, a social structure that provides too few rewarding aggressive outlets, and a television media that distorts the masculine identity by linking it to sexual promiscuity and unrestrained aggression.

A woman reared in the subservient mode will respond to criticism by going inward with self-blame or self-pity to avoid any retaliatory fantasies that might threaten the relationship. In the concept of "moral masochism," first proposed by Shapiro, a woman may persist indefinitely in her attempts to gain love despite any amount of abuse heaped upon her. Likewise, a well-trained German Shepherd will respond to abusive treatment by its master by licking the master's hand.

Self-concept is so dependent upon the relationship that anger is not a permissible option. When such a person is provoked to the point of tolerance breakdown, the decision will be made, not toward violence but toward capitulation and breaking down into tears, asking for forgiveness, or begging for mercy.

The above scenario is common in some homes in which the insecure man will persist in hostility, provoking his wife, children, or other family members with verbal abuse until they finally break down into tears, an endpoint that usually assuages his anger. Recently, the media has reported incidents of women who shoot or mutilate their abusing husbands. We can anticipate from this a dramatic increase in such incidents, now that the once forbidden door has been opened.

Battered wives learn to become adept at neutralizing the aggression inflicted by their emotionally disturbed and dysfunctional mates. However, this neutralizing never succeeds in alleviating abuse indefinitely.

In humans, a neurotic distortion of innate dominance-submissive tendencies may result in learned sadomasochistic behaviors wherein the dominant male feels compelled to bolster a shaky ego by repeatedly demonstrating his dominance over a scapegoat who has incorporated satisfying victim responses into his or her personality structure.

In nature, aggressive behavior usually diminishes rapidly when it does not meet resistance. Hence, "playing dead" may offer a salutary benefit. In humans, however, learned aggressive behavior is self-reinforcing, quickly becoming an habitual form of tension release.

A milder form of habitual aggressive discharge, all too common in family households, is characterized by verbal abuse, dumping, blaming, humiliating, and threatening to abandon the family. This behavior is almost always a learned pattern from an adult parent or authority figure within the household of origin.

In more serious situations in which physical abuse (again, a learned behavior) is involved, this physical abuse may eventuate into an addiction to violence. Once addicted to violent behavior, some men will begin purposely to distort or misperceive the conciliatory behavior of an habitual target in order to justify attack. And, here, passive submission may serve only to provoke more rage at being cheated of gratifying victim responses.

In most cases this pattern of violent behavior is self-contained within a given household. However, male children who have been victims of, or witness to, this type of emotional release through violent behavior, will often carry such behavior into the streets.

Solutions to the problem of community violence and street violence, which is gaining ever-increasing publicity, should focus on supporting the family unit and reducing family violence. Family violence can be reduced only by reducing stress on the male population by assuring men adequate opportunities to provide financial and emotional support to their wives and children. It is a sad fact that inadequate fathers often view their devoted wife and children as adversaries, and will attack them for their neediness.

Dr. Carl Bell, an African-American psychiatrist, writing for the *Psychiatric Times*, May, 1992, states: "Discussions of the 'homicide problem' in African-American communities most often focus on those that occur as a result of predatory violence, interracial homicide, the use of excessive force by police, and gang violence. Yet most African-American homicides result from expressive violence secondary to interpersonal conflict and, as a result, the home, not the street, is the primary location of African-American homicides. Clearly, an individual should have at least one place to feel safe." He adds: "This natural resource, i.e., a loving family, should not be overlooked as a buffer that neutralizes the effects of community violence."

Dr. Bell's statement should not be misconstrued to single out the African-American community, as it applies equally strongly to all ethnic groups that are forced into unnatural environments, lacking a sense of identification and respect from the greater society, and deprived of healthy options for attaining a sense of financial security and self-esteem.

D.H. Lawrence states this dilemma eloquently (quoted in *Celebrate the Solstice,* 1994): "...This is what is the matter with us, we are bleeding at the roots, because we are cut off from the earth and the sun and stars, and love is a grinning mockery, because, poor blossom, we plucked it from its stem on the tree of Life, and expected it to keep on blooming in our civilized vase on the table."

Chapter Seven

The Will-to-Power
and the Will-to-Serve

Humanity's survival depends on a redirection of the aggressive drive to humanistic, heroic, and moral endeavors. These options must be taught by our educational system and by the television media. The innate desire to serve in a special way, to rescue an endangered loved one by an act of heroism, even the willingness to sacrifice one's life for a patriotic cause is much more a characteristic of the human spirit than is the urge to seek recognition through an act of senseless violence.

In all humans there is an innate Will-to-Power, coupled with an innate Will-to-Serve.

> The Will-to-Power is motivated by the desire to control, gain, own, overcome obstacles and achieve praise through recognition, status, and power.

> The Will-to-Serve is the desire to admire, emulate, and to follow a strong leader and to gain praise through obedience.

The Will-to-Serve comes from a genuine desire to

establish a positive bond with a strong authority figure, to gain a sense of significance through
identification, and to earn praise through selfless obedience. This type of devotional bond to a person, a cause,
or a country brings a sense of fulfillment through service. Every successful politician and every major
non-profit organization in this country owes its success
to the dedication provided by individuals who receive
satisfaction through serving. Each country is beholden
to its patriots for its survival. The search for significance can lead to bonding to a political movement, a
cult, or a cause. The willingness to serve can be motivated by identifying with an imagined "good," such as
a "just" war.

The majority of people within any general population have a much stronger "will-to-serve" than "will-
to-power." The common anger expressed toward authority figures is usually the result of disillusionment. Born
leaders, bosses, and supervisors are hard to find. The
desire to follow a special leader or "guru" has led many
of our young adults into cults or radical religious
groups and into extremist political movements. *The
youth of this country would become much less of a
problem if the will-to-serve were properly reinforced
instead of the common practice of focusing attention
on the suppression of the will-to-power.*

We cannot overestimate the urge within all young
adults to seek a strong leader with whom to identify
and to follow. Almost any strong-willed individual with
an unswerving goal and a conviction in his rightness
will almost certainly be able to gather some followers
about him, regardless of his direction.

Despite the risks involved, especially in regard to the loss of personal freedom, a common way in which the general masses have chosen to resolve their mutual conflicts, historically, is to subordinate their will to a leader who appears to have all the right answers, and to follow him with unquestioning loyalty.

The Servitude Trap

There is a world of difference between unconditional obedience based on mutual respect and trust (i.e., devotional obedience) and subservient obedience attained through the destruction of one's identity and/or will. The first attains willing and enthusiastic compliance motivated by the expectation of praise. The latter attains mechanical servitude behaviors motivated by the fear of reprimand or physical harm. *Subservient behavior is defined as unquestioning compliance or obedience to a dominant figure in the absence of a bond of respect.* It is based on fear, a sense of hopelessness against all resistance, and a self-image that is compatible with the servitude role.

Most people born into slavery or a servitude status tend to alleviate their inner anxiety by adopting an attitude of blind obedience. This submissive, non-resistant, servitude mode was often very functional in the past for prolonging survival and obtaining favored positions of trust in master-slave relationships. An early decision from childhood, of unconditional obedience, makes this mode a permanent and predictable attitude, not open to hesitation or re-decision, and hence free from conflict. Dominant behavior by the master of the house is met automatically with subservient responses in order to minimize abusive aggression. The servitude trap is probably unknown in the animal kingdom. Here we are not referring merely to a pecking order, but to an ongoing unbalanced relationship in which one member is consistently benefited at the relative expense of the other. However, the phenomena of victimization, exploitation, suppression of ethnic minorities, and control through intimidation is a characteristic feature of the human condition.

Passive subservience to cruelty, such as wife-beating, must be imposed from birth. In the absence of any model of rebellion, it can succeed in suppressing the awakening of the will, and ingrain subservient behaviors into the self-image of the personality structure. Thus, serfs, scullery maids, and servants of aristocratic lords rarely rebelled or even considered rebellion as an option.

Abusive parents can have the same effect on their children. Sadly, I have worked with dozens of fairly well-functioning adults who came from extremely abusive families and who now have no access to their anger. They often present a friendly and happy appearance to cover the inner emptiness they feel. They have difficulty being aggressive in any line of work, and often become involved in abusive relationships. Those who are more dysfunctional may fall into heavy alcohol and substance abuse because they were never trained to have a disciplined mind serving a stable sense of self.

Unfortunately for the human race, women for many centuries and in most countries of the world have been trained by their mothers from birth to assume a sub-servient relationship to men. Until very recently in this century, the family hierarchy was fixed by religious as well as cultural tradition: the man served as the ulti-mate authority figure in the family. His decisions were not be questioned.

In those situations where there was some love and flexibility in the relationship, the woman learned to become an expert in the art of covert manipulation. She might use sex, tears, physical illness, subtle suggestion, or take advantage of her husband's many blind spots to assume some modicum of control in a situation. However, there were still more times than he knew, when she cried herself to sleep at night. Many women who have exhausted all options to maintain some sem-blance of self-respect express their rebellion by sinking into deep depression, and eventually leaving the physi-cal body, cancer usually being the preferred route.

The Politics of Obedience

In primitive societies where the chief or leader is held in high esteem, or in totalitarian societies ruled by an emperor, pharaoh, or king who rules by divine right, the majority of the population avoids inner con-flict by adopting an attitude of unconditional obedience.

Unconditional obedience is expected and demanded in a number of healthy relationship dyads including those of field commander-soldier, king-countryman, con-ductor-pianist, maestro-student, spiritual leader-disciple, coach-player, and ideally, parent-child. This is a highly efficient model for teaching, ruling, or waging war, because within it there is no friction, no energy-wasting pattern of power struggles, and relatively little need for dealing with disobedience because the dominant position of the leader is unquestioned.

But all this changes dramatically when contempt or disrespect arise on either side of the equation, regardless of the cause or the justification. (We see this in many of our inner-city public schools.) Now there exists inner questioning, passive or open resistance to orders, and the build-up of resentment that requires significant policing to discourage rebellion. *The use of physical punishment always denotes the failure of discipline. And discipline fails only when there is lack of mutual respect and trust.*

Punishment, or the threat of punishment, involving pain and/or prolonged physical confinement, is still believed to be an effective deterrent to rebellious behavior, as well as a way to insure future compliance. Instead, it results in promoting fear, resentment, and a sense of injustice which may actually compel a repetition of the forbidden behavior. Punishment significantly severs whatever bond may have existed between two parties, whether it be state and criminal or parent and child. Communication thereafter deteriorates to mechanical and subservient responses, masking simmering rage and the wish for revenge. This increases the need for vigilance, surveillance, and policing to insure obedience.

Dictatorships that are imposed on the people of a territory or state often try to win unconditional obedience by inflicting sufficiently severe and cruel punishment on every person who demonstrates an attitude of rebellion. Such an attempt relies on the mistaken belief that the will of the people will be broken when they come to realize that all resistance is useless. But this method of control can never be effective for long with a population that has tasted freedom, or has knowledge of other countries that live more happily under a model of benign leadership. Unfortunately, some parents run their family like a dictatorship, not realizing that with a bond of love and devotion, oppression and punishment become entirely unnecessary. When an insecure parent resorts to such means of control, his action represents a cruel misuse of power, an act of violence.

Democracies, on the other hand, are not dependent on unconditional obedience to a leader. Political figures are frequently criticized, second-guessed, and assailed by opponents and various advocate groups. The acceptance of expressions of protest through marches, free speech, letters to the editor, public forums, etc., helps to temper aggression by offering an outlet for frustration.

The system works as long as it is sustained by a respect for the system. The leader becomes less important than the system. When the people lose faith in the system, they oppose it in ways that promote aggression or disobedience of its laws.

A democracy is not structured to control a dissident population; only a dictatorship can do that. Thus, failed democracies, i.e., democracies that cannot sustain a viable economy or protect their citizens from violence, become vulnerable to the establishment of a dictatorship with the consent of the people.

The following graphs show how the relative balance between the will-to-power and the will-to-serve is influenced under different training environments:

A. Ideal development in an environment
   of mutual

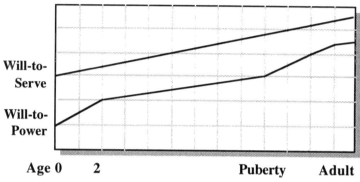

Will-to-Serve

Will-to-Power

Age 0   2   Puberty   Adult

The Will-to-Power grows steadily with time but always remains below the Will-to-Serve.

B.   In an atmosphere of deliberate punitive suppression.

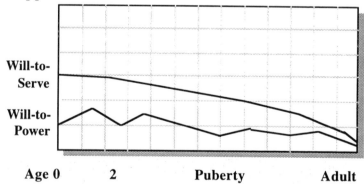

Will-to-Serve

Will-to-Power

Age 0   2   Puberty   Adult

Obedience with hidden resentment; a fermenting potential for violence.

C. In an atmosphere of catering or reverse dominance (sometimes called *"spoiling the child"*).

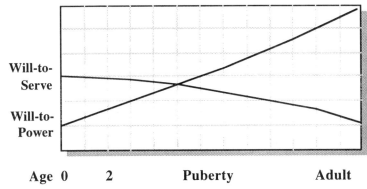

Age 0   2   Puberty   Adult

This results in a self-centered individual with contempt for others and a tendency to be tyrannical in a position of authority.

D. In societies raised in unconditional obedience. (Also seen in fanatical patriotism, cults, and street-gang identification.)

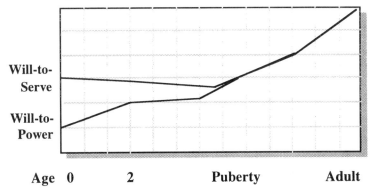

Age 0   2   Puberty   Adult

The Will-to-Serve becomes identified with the Will-to-Power. Glory in "dying for a cause."

E. Teenage Rebellion in a previously passive child, improperly handled by parent.

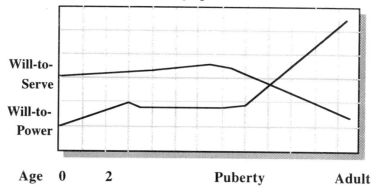

Age 0   2   Puberty   Adult

The Parents' rigid control pattern is overridden by peer pressure and the permissive social model of today.

F. Unpopular dictatorship, i.e., control in the hands of a different ethnic minority.

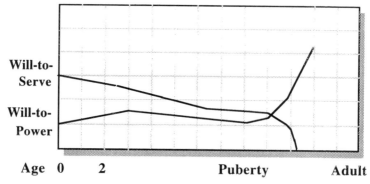

Age 0   2   Puberty   Adult

There may be a wide variance between Will-to-Power and Will-to-Serve for a relatively long period of time before the "sudden" outbreak of violence.

Chapter Eight

The Performance Trap

Why is it that humans are not more happy? Why is the human condition so beset with fear, turmoil, and a feeling of being overwhelmed? It isn't that we don't have intelligence. Humans have been gifted with a brain that has allowed them to dominate all other life forms on this planet.

Perhaps it is because of the direction we have chosen to focus our consciousness. Human beings are caught up in an endless search for significance through performance, being driven to attain more admiration, more praise, or more wealth than anyone else. The major contenders drive themselves to keep pursuing this elusive goal by beating themselves with guilt, self-reproach and blame. Reaching a materialistic goal in our society has become more important than the methods used to get there.

Each society places its own value judgments on what attributes or talents are to be praised and rewarded. In ancient Greece, for example, a philosophical thinker might be held in esteem, whereas in ancient Sparta or Rome, a sturdy and fearless warrior might be the popular choice for awards. We might assume that during the Renaissance period in Europe, musical and artistic talent gained high recognition, as did literature and poetry in Elizabethan England.

Today artists and poets, with rare exception, are not members of a thriving profession. For the past 50 years, increasing value and emphasis has been placed on a test measurement called I.Q. developed in the early part of this century. This test, essentially, measures the capacity of the left brain to act like a computer in storing, retrieving and analyzing words and symbols. The speed at which the brain does this is of prime consideration in the scoring. Scoring has less value if its limitations are recognized. The I.Q. test does not attempt to measure the creative, artistic, intuitive talents generally attributed to the right brain, and from which all of our noblest achievements in music, literature, and scientific discoveries have come.

The push for scholastic performance in our generation begins at an increasingly early age. With this is the promotion of competition for technological skills which gradually closes down the right brain and, with it, an identification with nature and spiritual values. The outer world becomes more real than the inner.

We are taught in school, the first time we are old enough to compete in a spelling bee, that there are winners and losers. In our school system, the name of the game is competition. Grading is often based on a curve. Students are tested and re-tested to meet state and national norms to justify the jobs of the administrators of the school system.

Basically, this shows who is best at short-term memorizing of reams of rote information and regurgitating it on demand in a prescribed way. The same small group of students keep winning all the awards, medals, honors, and scholarships. Those who win are not to be envied. Success carries its own special trap. The win is exhilarating, but temporary. The need for an encore begins immediately, to re-establish proof of significance by beating the old mark.

A sad example of this fact is illustrated by one of my friends in high school, whom I shall call David. David was an over-achiever who won almost every academic contest he entered. I both admired and envied him. Initially we were competitors, but it soon became clear to me that there was no contest because I was either unwilling or unable to discipline myself to invest the energy he was willing to put into winning. He maintained a 4.0 average and was also a gifted cello player.

In our junior year of high school he won the state spelling contest against all other high school contestants. That evening he called me on the telephone to announce his success. I did not recognize at the time that he was not meaning to be boastful, but rather was making a desperate attempt to reach out for love and respect. The high school principal, the next day, called a brief student assembly to acknowledge the honor he brought to our school. Yet only in retrospect do I realize how lonely he was. Other students tended to ignore or to resent him.

After graduation David went to Yale and I never saw him again. However, a year later I did receive from him a newspaper clipping that had appeared in his hometown paper, acknowledging that he was the top student in the freshman class that year. A couple of years later I inquired about him to a mutual friend. He answered, "Didn't you hear about David?" On a trip to New York City David had slashed his wrists and jumped from a ten-story building. This news had a profound effect on me, as if David had fallen victim to a form of disease which I, myself, had narrowly missed.

As a psychiatrist I became interested in treating suicidal adolescents. From my own work and from reading the literature on teenage suicides I came to see that David's case was not unique. It is often the highest achiever, the most successful and gifted high school student, who suddenly takes his life. I have interviewed many of them who seriously attempted suicide by various means but had failed.

Each one talked about their sense of overwhelm, their inability to keep up the competitive pace, and the despair of what they faced ahead of them in maintaining a high status level at the major college that their father had selected for them.

Brian is a characteristic example. He was referred to me after he calmly, and without much prior consideration, took ten of his mother's sleeping pills before going to bed. He did not even leave a suicide note because he wasn't quite sure what to put on it. He was surprised to wake up the next day, because he had underestimated the lethal dose. He then told his mother about the attempt, which prompted his referral to me.

Brian was not enthusiastic about talking about the incident. He appeared more apathetic than depressed, and somewhat disappointed that the suicide attempt had failed. He stared at the goldfish in my aquarium and said: "Why can't life be like that? There's no pressure on them to do anything."

Brian was scholastically at the top of his high school

class and was also a top-ranked tennis player. But life, for him, seemed insipid. He felt alone, confused, and directionless. His father was largely absent, attending his own successful law practice, but would occasionally come to see Brian's tennis matches. Brian was being pushed for a tennis scholarship at Stanford, but in the national high school finals he had met some of the gifted players who planned to attend Stanford, and he dreaded the work it would take to maintain their level of competitiveness. He had come to realize that he was doing it only to gain his father's love, and that somehow it all wasn't worth it.

I do not have the statistics on this, but I have never met a suicidal teenager or even a delinquent teenager who had the love of a strong, supportive father figure in the home! A large percentage of homes in our country today have the absence of a strong masculine presence, which affects adversely the mother as well as the children. What this observation signifies to me is that the war on drugs, the war on crime, the war on school dropouts, and the war on street gangs and violence must begin, and cannot be won without, the establishment of a responsible fathering role for all men in our society.

It might come as a surprise to consider that teenagers, as a group, are the most alienated from society. They serve no useful role or purpose. From early childhood and throughout the most vital and creative period of their lives they have been warehoused in sterile square rooms with 30 or more other students, and fed an endless stream of information that is completely irrelevant to what is really going on in their lives, in their homes, and in the streets where they live. They are offered little or no opportunity to find a sense of significance based on a meaningful role in society.

The most dehumanizing aspect of segregating 30 boys and girls in one room is that children are not homogeneous either in size, looks, rate of maturation, or modes of learning. Some children are visual learners, some are auditory learners, and a significant percentage, mostly boys, are motoric learners, which means that they have difficulty encoding information when their hands are not actively involved in the input. They tend to be restless, become behavior problems or daydream their way through the day. They feel like misfits and have a strong dislike for school. Similarly, the creative right-brained children are forced to limit themselves to the more tedious, less satisfying mode of linear learning of rote information, and have difficulty doing well even when "gifted."

Put yourself into the head of almost any teenager today and you will find little sense of personal power. Instead you will find confusion, insecurity, a sense of isolation, of alienation from society, and frustration at every level due to the blocked expression of pent-up aggressive, emotional, and sexual energies. Behind it all is a deeper spiritual hunger that the school system is not permitted to address.

The value placed on the three-dimensional world is such that one's identity becomes synonymous with physical appearances and possessions. By becoming identified with performance, people become entrapped in an isolated area of relative excellence so that the quality of life is lost. Enrico Caruso said, at one point in his life, that he felt trapped by his voice. People, everywhere, wanted to hear it and he had to go along.

The loneliness of the wife of the male achiever is legend. A man's self-concept becomes tied to a limited area in which he excels and upon which he may base his entire identity. I know of many quality physicians who spend long hours in surgery and in patient care and hospital visitation to the neglect of their family because they feel a greater sense of importance, and have a more clearly defined role, in a hospital setting than as a father or husband in the home setting. In this pattern of behavior, however, the quality of life is lost through demand for an unsustainable performance that often shortens their life.

The anxiety over performance can even take the enjoyment out of sex as illustrated by a disclosure made to me by one of the charismatic student leaders of the 1960's Free Speech Movement. He found himself pursued by numerous women who saw him as an outspoken, arrogant, masculine sex symbol. He confided to me that he had been forced into celibacy because he was afraid of being unable to perform according to expectations, and he did not want word to get around that "JR is a lousy lay."

Nothing captures an individual in the dehumanizing performance trap more than success. Japan provides an excellent example of the performance trap resulting in a high rate of teenage suicides. Once one of the most artistic and creative people in the world, the Japanese have shifted almost entirely to their left brain, becoming transformed symbolically into hamsters turning a giant money wheel, with no time off for rest on weekends or holidays. Meanwhile, they berate the United States for "being lazy," which really means that we are less driven into putting so much time and energy into pursuing a sense of significance that takes precedence over pain, pleasure, or even long-term physical survival.

I have treated a number of intelligent, talented and attractive young, single adults who are so stressed by their highly competitive work situations that they are relieved to escape to the solace of their barren apartments each evening, rarely socializing or taking the time for recreation. In their escape from a stressful world, they experience a sense of relief that makes them unaware of how lonely and sterile their lives really are.

Flower Children of the 60's

My psychiatric residency in the early 1960's at Langley Porter Neuropsychiatric Institute, next to the University of California Medical Center in San Francisco, provided an almost perfect timing and location for me to study the phenomenon of the growth of "Flower Children," or "Hippies," who had become increasingly entrenched in the nearby Haight-Ashbury District of the city.

The initial influx consisted of largely middle class and upper middle class young adults who sought an alternative to the successful and affluent life styles of their parents. Their own lives had been comfortably carved out for them in the established order, to succeed their fathers in a lucrative business occupation. It was no coincidence that the Hippie phenomenon began with the discovery and general use of drugs, such as LSD.

I enjoyed mingling informally on the street corners with this friendly population, out of a natural curiosity to explore the motives that had driven them to this kind of existence. Although they did not all state it in exactly these words, many of them openly shared with me that as a result of an hallucinogenic experience they were able to gain a higher perspective of consciousness and of life, and could see the shallow existences that their parents lived behind a sham of pretense.

The hallucinogenic experience offered them insight into the world of their parents, a highly predictable and mechanical existence essentially devoid of any real love or real happiness. Little time was set aside for precious moments of inner atunement and contemplation of the meaning and purpose of life.

These young people tried to explain that their parents, in the wild pursuit of establishing social esteem and success, rarely appeared to be at peace with themselves. This was evidenced by the fact that it didn't "feel good," to be around them. Their parents acted as if they had "no place of peace to go to in their heads."

These young adults who had been preened to follow in their parents' footsteps were instead trying to "feel good," even if that meant "spacing out." A few of them articulated with words such as seeking "inner wisdom," or "higher truth." However, none appeared really sure where they were going. They were clear only in that they wanted to change the direction in which their parents were pushing them.

They could see that their parents lived a life of pretense: over-stressed fathers pretending to be in total control, and depressed mothers pretending to be happy. It was not a pleasurable experience for these people to converse with parents who were so out of touch with their true motives and feelings that all they had to offer were pithy aphorisms. In contrast, they found a real sense of significance in the greeting that eventually became a trademark of the Hippie subculture: "Say it like it is, man."

The Establishment Trap

Another trap we fall into, as our society grows, is the trap of large corporations and establishments. To be able to focus our energies in a powerful and satisfying way, we must feel confident, certain, and convinced of the righteousness of our actions. However, this attitude can lead to extreme rigidity in thinking, rigidity that is deemed necessary to maintain a sense of security. This security is further strengthened by creating a strong organization that consists solely of like-minded individuals. There is a tendency to become entrapped within complex establishments that were initially constructed as building blocks to higher levels of organized growth, but which have instead become ossified barriers to further progress.

Just as a lobster must periodically be willing to shed its shell in order to grow, even if such shedding means a period of terrible vulnerability until the new becomes solidified, we should be willing periodically to look at all our beliefs and premises from a new perspective.

However, the left brain of humans finds security in holding tightly to its own "facts" and "truths" as barnacles hold tightly to the hull of a ship. In a quest for security, one may attack all progressive ideas as "heresy," or, "unorthodox." The intellect's security is predicated on protecting its established belief system.

This principle is the reason for the progressive rigidity of all social institutions and the power behind ritualistic practices.

Sigmund Freud before his death stated that his own Psychoanalytic Institute had become so rigid that he would not be allowed to remain a member if his name were not Freud. Part of the rigidity that is so common in our institutionalized establishments comes from the mistaken belief that any flexibility or wavering conviction on the part of the people in power will result in a weakening of their personal power. Additionally, there is fear that acceptance of any new ideas from outside the establishment will empower others who are not part of the establishment, and who are assumed to become a threat to the power base that is committed to the past.

The fear that solidly entrenched institutions, political power bases, and most people in a position of high authority may lose their dominant status if they permit any aggressive expression, or sign of power from the subordinated or lower classes, is one of the primary causes of social turmoil and upheaval. Certainly, permissiveness might eventually result in a narrowing of the disparity between the two levels in terms of material wealth and privileges, but this change occurs to the ultimate betterment of both if it is done in the spirit of acceptance and respect.

The Welfare Trap

We must recognize the inherent need in all healthy individuals to find a sense of significance and fulfillment through some type of performance or activity that makes a contribution to others, as well as to themselves. Of all the traps the population of a growing society can fall into, and by far the most deadly, is the trap born of a lack of opportunity for performance, especially within the context of a materialistic society.

A healthy society fills the needs of its citizens, protects them from harm, and provides ample opportunities for attaining a sense of significance through the expression of talent and playing of satisfying roles within the structure. For any adult, satisfying and remunerative work is a primary determinant for a personal sense of significance.

In a democracy, significance is largely dependent on personal performance. The challenge for personal growth, achievement, status, and security are all placed on one's own talents and motivations. Devotion is to self first, and to the organization second. This order of priority can result in considerable growth, and considerable selfishness as well.

Civilizations, as they grow more complex, place increasingly more demands upon their citizens to find a place, and to make a contribution, in order to remain a participant in the sharing of its productivity. As the social structure becomes more complex, more competitive, and more technological, increasingly large segments of the population fall into the category of the inept, those who represent a drain, rather than a resource to the society.

A study of history will suggest that the survival of every great civilization was largely dependent on its ability to care for the growing population of those citizens relegated to the category of inept. The core structure of a civilization depends on its willingness and its capacity to meet the needs and to integrate within its structure the various groups of people who are unable to compete within the structure without special assistance from the system. While we all have different capabilities and talents, the opportunity for expression of those talents is not equally available to all. The dissatisfaction of the unemployed festers as a sickness at the core. As the gap widens between the privileged and the deprived, a tolerance breakdown occurs that eventually leads to civil violence.

Giving money and food stamps is not the answer. The more you help, the more you encourage helplessness. Enabling only perpetuates weakness, and postpones the collapse of an unworkable situation. Instead, there must be a fundamental change in the conditions that now foster a feeling of victimization, a pattern of servitude, and a sense of alienation.

Everyone has a need for a special place or role in the social order:

A place to rule: a place where people have a sense of personal power, and

A place to serve: an area in which people can make a personal contribution.

The Retirement Trap

In later life, senior citizens who have reached the retirement they worked so long to attain complain of a loss of identity and sense of significance in our society.

Psychiatrist Mary Bishop, in her 70's and semi-retired since 1976, comments on the loss of self-worth in both younger and older retirees. "People tend to wrap their careers around them, flouting their positions like splendid clothes. They felt vital, needed, and competent in their careers. People sought them out for advice. They got paid for what they did. They had a certain amount of power over others and over their lives. Then, they retired and fell off the significance meter."

Humans, like animals that are maintained in an untenable environment, have the capacity to surrender the life force and die when their life becomes meaningless. The sad part is that in reality our senior citizens are in a position to understand a whole new meaning to life based on spiritual values, but most cannot rise above their limited identity with their former work role which, when lost, all too often leaves them with little justification for their existence.

Chapter Nine

Management of
Juvenile Delinquents

A reprimand is a mild form of attack, which stirs the survival instinct into resentment. Any approach to establish dominance by intimidating the survival instinct of another person must progressively increase the level of punishment and threats in order to maintain control over the rising level of anger that this practice incites. *Whenever dominance is maintained by force, there is always a high risk of rebellion or violence, even though this appears unlikely at the time.*

If our prison system is to have any therapeutic value other than punishment as a deterrent to crime, it must adopt structured programs that shift the attitudes of inmates away from seeking a sense of significance through rebellion and violence, to a new direction that gains self-esteem through mastery. We can end violence only through empowerment, not punishment.

However, we do not want to make the mistake of reinforcing a performance trap that is motivated only by achievement. Rather, praise must be directed toward attitude, the willingness to cooperate, the desire to please, and the acceptance of the other person's position of authority without provocation or challenge. This attitude must be, as much as possible, a free will decision if it is to earn legitimate praise. This requires that optional choices, such as "No," are subject to minimal, unemotional consequences, and never to physical punishment or humiliation.

This sounds simplistic, but does it work in practice? I had an impressive first-hand opportunity to observe the praise-versus-reprimand philosophy applied to a group of adolescents who were incarcerated in the California Youth Authority and who were pre-screened for an Intensive Treatment Program because of the severity of their social and emotional problems. Nearly all were charged with multiple violations including arson, rape, armed robbery, assault, and murder. Additionally, many were labeled "incorrigible" at school, at home, in the juvenile halls, and in the group homes where they had previously been placed.

All psychiatrists receive extensive training in uncovering the root causes of depressed feelings and low self-esteem. We learn how to offer ourselves for the healing experience as caring, objective listeners, who allow and accept the gradual verbal release of emotional tension, and who patiently examine very personal trauma in a safe setting.

But relatively few psychiatrists receive extensive training in handling violent, rebellious, and out-of-control behavior in which all of the pent-up frustration, rage, and self-hate are "acted-out," instead of just talked about. In the short term, such an individual is usually hospitalized and heavily medicated until all the stirred-up biological processes come to rest and rational thinking is restored. Then, ideally, the patient will continue with follow-up outpatient therapy to learn how to cope with his feelings by communicating them verbally and by finding more acceptable outlets to prevent their future build-up. But what about the thousands of teenagers and young adults who are unwilling or unable to communicate their feelings, and instead have chosen violence as a way of life?

My decision to accept a position as the psychiatrist in an Intensive Treatment Program for disturbed adolescents with the California Youth Authority proved to be an invaluable learning experience for me. I had just completed ten years as Medical Director of a large, multipurpose center for handicapped children and adults in Contra Costa County. In this setting, the love and attention given to these children had, of itself, a high therapeutic value. I left convinced from this experience that love, or the lack of it, can dramatically affect a child's I.Q.

But love was definitely not enough when it came to juvenile criminals incarcerated for a variety of violent crimes that included assault, rape, armed robbery, and murder. These young people had all closed themselves off long ago to the pain of not being loved, and were not ready to again put any value or trust upon overtures of love or caring. Additionally they were filled with self-hate, which imposed an impassable barrier to the acceptance of love.

The majority came from chaotic, dysfunctional, and abusive homes where language was rarely used for rational communication. The spoken word was used primarily to coerce, intimidate, seduce, control, or otherwise evoke terror and submission. All of this behavior, invoked at an impressionable age, damages a child's self-concept into believing that this is what he deserves.

He will side with the rejecting parent into hating himself. *There is no greater destructive force in the universe than a man who hates himself.*

Most of the wards felt empty emotionally and saw life as an endless series of problems without solutions. They did not have much hope of changing themselves or bettering their condition. Their underlying anger was so intense that it blocked verbalization of their thoughts. Their feelings and needs had never been integrated into a rational self-dialogue. Instead, these young people preoccupied themselves with fantasies of "pay-back" and revenge as a self-healing process, i.e., as a way of maintaining some sense of significance.

These youths had been deprived of the basic essentials of early training and discipline and, consequently, had never developed a disciplined mind and had no respect for authority. The question most people might have is, "Is it too late?" In fact, there is some pressure from the general population to extend prison terms and inflict stronger punishments as the only realistic way to protect society at this point.

In a real sense, these youthful criminals were much like unsocialized animals, and any discipline, to be effective, had to start at the most elementary level, as if we were dealing with children below the age of three or four years. We were able to do this because we had the resources, in this setting, to enforce our limits physically, in the same way that parents do with young children. Generally, the fewer the number and the more simple the means of enforcement, the more effective.

We used primarily two modes for compliance: room restriction and temporary soft restraints. Both the imposition and the length of time of these controls was directly related to the ward's behavior. And as with children, coercion, infliction of pain, threats, and reprimand would lead only to rebellion and power struggles, while catering, bribery, and leniency would lead to disrespect and constant limit testing.

Fortunately the administrator of the Intensive Treatment Unit, Dewey Willis, was a man of considerable experience and had a caring heart for these wards. He set up a highly structured program that implemented, step-by-step, the basic principles of behavior management:

1. Establish yourself in the position of authority.
2. Be consistent.
3. Use praise rather than punishment or blame.

It was crucial to establish our position of authority immediately. There was no question that we were in a position of control in the jail-house setting; however, the way in which we exercised that control had everything to do with outcome. Basic rules and limits were clearly set and communicated, not only by the staff, but by other wards who had earned leadership positions in the program. This basic orientation proved helpful in reducing the fear that comes with feeling helpless in a controlling situation.

Expectedly, there would follow a period of days to weeks of aggressive attempts by the new ward to challenge our authority by defying and testing each of the limits. This testing included a range of behaviors such as profanity, verbal threats, refusal to follow schedules, banging the walls of their room, cracking the look-in window to their room, destroying property, setting fire to their bed, making suicidal gestures and, less often, actually assaulting or attempting to assault other wards and staff. The most destructive behaviors were kept at a minimum through constant staff surveillance and by safe-proofing the environment so that no valuable property or equipment was left exposed to theft or damage. Each behavior was met with a consistent, predictable, unemotional response.

"Unemotional" is the key word here. An emotional charge put on any communication in a situation of supervision, or from any position of power, has the effect of transforming a correction into a reprimand. A correction is a reminder or a gentle prompting to keep someone on a prescribed course, while a reprimand is an expression of displeasure at willful disobedience. At best, it implies stupidity or ignorance and promotes a sense of guilt, defensiveness, and inferiority.

All too often parents with their children, teachers with their students, and bosses with their employees enforce their authority with a tone of reprimand. This practice may temporarily appear to succeed in promoting servitude responses. However, especially in the absence of prior positive bonding, it prompts inner resentment or an aggressive counter-response and, in any case, closes off open communication.

Any tone of reprimand on the part of the youth counselor, while in the process of reaffirming a limit, would be misinterpreted as degrading or punitive and would trigger the counter-aggressive and survival instincts that these youngsters had learned to maintain at a high state of reactivity. Moreover, once these wards saw that they had the ability to trigger an emotional reaction of any sort (which in the jail-house vernacular is called, "getting hooked"), they knew how to escalate the interaction into a heavy game of counter-manipulation and an energy-draining power struggle. The ward would declare a "win" if he succeeded in upsetting the counselor or, even better, prompting him to over react inappropriately so as to set himself up for a disciplinary review by the administrator.

As long as the defined limits remained unemotionally inflexible, resistance against them diminished. But the slightest inconsistency by the staff could lead to endless hassling by the wards, i.e., "I was only five minutes late," or "I couldn't get up for breakfast because I couldn't get to sleep last night," or, "I whacked him because he wouldn't get out of my face!" "I'm wearing these pants 'cause my regulation pants don't fit me," etc., etc. On the other hand, no one hassles with the law of gravity, which is both unforgiving and very dependable.

Once the wards accepted the futility of resistance, they began noticeably to relax. It was as if they recognized the fact that limits worked both ways. The presence of a strong authority in control was now protecting them from abuse and attack. In this setting they no longer needed to keep their survival mechanisms in a high state of alert, as they did on the streets from which they came. Unwilling conformity actually became a way of letting go of a heavy load of internal instability and emotional conflict. This transition often occurred surprisingly smoothly because there was no power struggle, hence, no sense of defeat or humiliation.

On the contrary, for the first time in his life, the ward felt able to experience a sense of security in knowing that he was in total control of the specific responses he received from the staff. Until now these youngsters had no idea how their actions affected others. They saw the behavior of others as being totally inner directed, not related to their own behavior, and something beyond their control. Now, they began to develop an "observing ego," which is the ability to stand back and watch the interaction from both sides. They could now substitute the sense of power they felt in "hooking" the other person, for the power of eliciting favorable responses. This predictable action-response pattern with their counselor soon began to establish a security bond to him, and with it, a bond of respect. Now, each compliance had more and more an element of willingness to it.

The slightest willingness to comply was then rewarded with praise. *Note that it was the willingness, not the performance, that was praised.* We were reinforcing and conditioning an attitude that could slowly develop into a stronger, positive bond. The willing attitude was also rewarded with increasing privileges such as having a radio in their room, being allowed to stay up late to watch television in the recreation room, etc.

The program was structured so that a ward could move up four levels of increasing privileges, responsibility, and leadership as he earned them. Rising through these levels depended on willingness to maintain a disciplined mind in school performance, personal hygiene, work assignments, therapy groups, and recreational activities. With this willingness came the ability to be a role model to the other wards.

These opportunities for mastery and recognition had a powerful, built-in, self-motivating force because of their associated positive enhancement to self-concept. Also, making available an opportunity to move up the pecking order in any structured system significantly reduces anger and the sense of helplessness. Aggressive energy can now be channeled into self-improvement. The average stay in the treatment program was one year. It was truly amazing to see the changes some of the wards made during this time, not only in personal self-care and relationship behaviors, but also in supporting and counseling the newer wards. I remember fondly one particular young man, Steve, who was taken from his parents at an early age because of severe abuse, and raised in foster homes where he continued to experience various forms of physical and emotional abuse. He was almost illiterate and had never learned to articulate his needs and his feelings. Anger was the only emotion with which he identified. He escaped from his inner void and feelings of fear by finding outside targets for his hate. The only way he knew how to find any sense of significance was to create chaos in his environment, and thus become the focus of major upset and concern by the caretakers and the authority figures who had assumed responsibility for him. His behavior was much like that of a wild, caged animal when he first came to the unit.

I first met Steve when I rushed from my office to investigate a loud ruckus coming from the day room. I arrived at the time Steve was being dragged by three counselors into his room, fiercely kicking and biting, despite the fact that a fourth security guard was standing by with a can of mace. It required the four to tie him down on his bunk with soft restraints while he struggled wildly, and let out loud threats and curses.

I talked with his counselor, who was a man with

considerable experience and competence but who acknowledged that he was dumbfounded by this ward's
almost daily unprovoked outbursts of disruptive and
combative behavior. He asked whether I could evaluate
Steve for some type of schizophrenic disorder.

I entered Steve's room, where he continued to curse
and bite on his leather restraints, and calmly asked him
if he would like to have a cup of coffee with me when
he got tired of playing this game. I felt that his response to this offer would provide me with some
valuable information about him. He reactively attacked
me verbally with words such as: "Get the F_ _ _ out
of here you crazy M _ _ _ _ _ F _ _ _ _ _ _ shrink."
I left quietly and returned to my office. About ten
minutes later Steve began calling for me to see him.
This time he looked much more in control of himself
and greeted me with: "That cup of coffee sounds pretty
good."

It was with considerable reluctance that the counselors finally agreed to release Steve's shackles and to let
him sit with me at a table in the corner of the day-
room. I brought some coffee from my personal
coffee-maker in my office, and we talked for almost
an hour. He appeared elated at the attention I was
giving him.

He recounted his experience of being placed by his
mother in one foster home after another. The only way
he could keep from getting depressed was to find someone to hate and to keep up an ongoing state of tension
with that person. His mother never came to visit him
except when he created a major crisis and the social
worker ordered her to attend a meeting to decide on
his next placement.

I made an agreement with Steve to have a talk with him whenever his counselor told me that he had had a good day. Over the next year there was not a single recurrence of Steve's disruptive behavior. On the contrary, he became more interested in learning to read and to write so that he could write down his life story for me as I had suggested. He began assuming more and more responsibilities and, despite the fact that he had low average intelligence and a residual attention deficit disorder, he slowly rose up the phase structure to a status involving some leadership and special privileges.

Steve had never known of any way to earn praise for his behavior. But once given the opportunity, he responded to praise like a plant that turns its leaves to the sun. His transformation into a leader, over the year he was in the Wintu Lodge, is a real tribute to the praise vs. reprimand approach. This structured setting demonstrated the indisputable fact that praise is always a much stronger motivating factor than reprimand, and that behavior is strongly related to environmental conditioning.

I wish I could conclude with a more positive ending to this story. However, statistical follow-ups indicate that the majority of even the most improved wards, once they returned to their unstructured and dehumanizing home environments, revert to their previous delinquent behaviors. Environmental conditioning without continuous positive support is difficult, if not impossible, for most individuals to overcome.

I have not seen Steve since his release some ten years ago. But I never tried to seek a follow-up on his status for fear of what I might learn, since I had become quite attached to him during his year of rapid growth. Yet, despite all of his progress, he was still ill-equipped to handle the challenges of the outer world, given the inadequate support system we now have.

Chapter Ten

Evaluating the Motives for Disruptive Behavior

Naturalists who study the behavior of animals, birds, and insects have arrived at some clearly defined and predictable patterns of each species around feeding, mating, raising the young, and making adaptive responses to the environment. Human behavior, on the surface, appears to be far more complex, but if we reduce the variables by focusing on the category of socially acceptable (conforming) versus socially unacceptable (non-conforming) behaviors, we can make some useful observations.

Behavior, from its simplest definition, is a definable activity or action. Our attitudes and our reactions to the particular behavior of others are colored by the subjective judgments we make regarding the motives that prompted the behavior. Once we label a behavior as "willful disobedience," "insane," "manipulative," "uncaring," "hostile," "selfish," etc., we then react to the label and to the "attitude" that usually fits that label. For example, a child may spill milk on the floor and the parents will react according to their interpretation, ranging from "innocent accident," or "careless indifference," to "an act of defiance."

Most of the arguments between married couples are due to the negative misinterpretation of motives, and to the counterattacks that result from being wrongly accused. It requires considerable training to refrain from projecting one's own insecurity and motives upon the behavior of others and to assume a totally objective stance. This is, of course, more easily accomplished with animals than with children, but even here emotionalism can often interfere with training.

Every society establishes its own set of rules regarding the proper expression of social behaviors, so as to avoid misinterpretation. These rules become part of the customs and norms of the society. They represent a consensus as to what constitutes appropriate or polite behavior, eccentric but acceptable behavior, or deviant, non-conforming, and unacceptable behavior. *A behavior is labeled as aggressive behavior whenever it results in making an uninvited impact upon the environmental space of another person.* The result is usually some degree of annoyance, even when it's only giving to someone an unanticipated hug. This annoyance may not even be directed at you. A child's loud talking or screaming in a restaurant may elicit feelings of annoyance, rising gradually to anger, especially if you tell yourself that the behavior is "entirely inappropriate" and, furthermore, "the result of poor parenting."

All living organisms have a natural propensity to express, periodically, innate aggressive patterns of behavior, even in the form of play. In general, the more civilized the culture, the more restricting and limited are aggressive options against any type of interpersonal provocation. Society decides which aggressive behaviors are justifiable and which are not. For example, in some countries the social order may sympathize with your shooting a man you find in bed with your wife; however, you are not permitted to punch his nose for taking your parking space.

The outer world is always in opposition to our will, even in a "free society." We are always struggling with the inner option of conformance versus rebellion. Every stable culture instills in its citizenry habits, rituals, and customs, behaviors that lead to comfortable, mechanically appropriate interactions within the population. As long as this practice includes a sense of security, adequate opportunities to maintain a livelihood, and a sense of justice, the likelihood for outbreaks of violence will be minimized.

Thus, management of aggression in a way that maintains the security of the territorial boundaries of each individual member is the primary task of every democracy, every superintendent of a school, institution, or prison, every military commander, and every head of a family. Aggression, improperly contained, provokes counter-aggression, and eventually violence.

Aggressive Patterns Are Linked to Play

Patterns of aggression that are innate in every animal are not automatically linked to hostile emotions or destructive goals. In fact, these patterns form the basis for play activities such as chasing, running away, wrestling, etc. In humans these patterns may be refined, with practice, into specialized skills used in sports, such as basketball, football, tennis, and recreational activities such as dancing.

Aggressive behavior in mammals consists of a relatively coordinated series of movements that can be evoked by stimulating the brain in the area of the hypothalamus. Such movements include stalking, biting, seizing, shaking, etc. These are stereotyped reactions to a variety of stimuli such as odor, color, rapid movement, or impingement on the animal's territory by a foreign animal. Aggression is an innate behavioral mechanism governing primarily the patterns of attack for purposes of gaining food. It must be stressed that this behavior is mechanical, unconscious, impersonal, and relatively consistent and predictable in each species.

In carnivorous animals, such as the large cat, aggressive attack patterns against a prey for food purposes is made without warning and with relatively little emotion on the part of the attacker. A different mechanism is involved when the animal's territory is invaded. The animal gives a warning sound, such as a hiss, to alert the intruder that his alarm system is on. If the intruder leaves, the alarm system subsides and the aggressive pattern is avoided.

Defensive Patterns Are Linked to Violence

If the intruder is a larger animal who persists in invasive behavior, then a full-blown defensive pattern may be triggered. The cat's body will stiffen up, the hairs on its back will rise, and its hissing increase in an attempt to discourage further aggression. Anger and rage reactions are now triggered which overcome fear, and which mobilize the body to sustain an attack.

Again, this response is designed to discourage aggression or to defend against it, and does not have violence as its aim.

Whereas defensive emotions in animals quickly die down unless they are continually fed, anger and rage in humans are perpetuated by angry thoughts that fester and build up in intensity over time, without any additional stimulation. In animals, anger and rage subside when the immediate threat is removed. But humans will continue to nurse indefinitely the feelings of humiliation and personal insult, and will fantasize opportunities for revenge long after the event that triggered these feelings, until the urge for violence, given appropriate weapons, becomes irresistible. Thus, a pattern that in nature is limited to defensive purposes in the face of imminent threat becomes, in humans, a justification for unrestrained and premeditated violence.

How the Mind Influences Anger

What may appear to an observer as senseless violence always makes sense to the perpetrator. With rare exceptions, violence is always premeditated and perceived as justifiable behavior. Even when it appears to be the result of sudden provocation, the violent act is always previously rehearsed, over and over, in the mind of the perpetrator awaiting the proper justification for expression.

Because of this built-in sense of righteousness, it is extremely rare for a perpetrator of violence to experience any real remorse for the victim, even years later. On the contrary, rehearsing the incident in the mind later often reactivates the original feelings of violence and the desire to repeat it. Given the same set of circumstances again, we can predict that the act will be repeated, be it wife-beating or murder.

Freud's Theory on Violence

Sigmund Freud based his original theories of behavior on the instincts governing pain and pleasure. However, when World War I broke out he was at a loss to explain the wanton bloodshed he witnessed. This led him to postulate another instinct, which he labeled "thanatos," the death instinct.

It is amazing to me how he could have missed the obvious: War is not the result of any natural instinct. War is the result of man's reasoning mind! It is man's reasoning mind that makes him far more dangerous than any other mammal, and far more destructive to himself, his neighbors, and to the planet. His reasoning mind is quite capable of convincing itself to kill millions of other people as a service to God!

Only in recent years have we become aware of the capacity of the average person to commit acts of aggression when following the orders of a person in authority. Adolph Eichmann, who masterminded the holocaust that resulted in the death of millions of Jews in World War II, was kidnapped by the Israeli secret service, Mossad, and taken to Israel in 1962. There he was administered a battery of psychological tests with surprising results. He passed as perfectly normal in every respect, including attitudes toward family and social mores.

Since that time a number of research studies have shown that volunteers will readily give excruciatingly painful shocks to innocent subjects at the command of the person in charge. The lesson to be learned here is that even "normal" aggression can be lethal if misdirected and not restrained by a sense of personal conscience. Reports by Amnesty International reveal how willing many people are to surrender their conscience to an authority figure, and to torture other people as "part of a day's work."

While animals are feeling-instinctive by nature, humans alone are thinking, willing, and feeling beings. Yet when the feeling aspect, so basic to the animal nature, is insidiously deleted by society while leaving the thinking and willing aspect intact, then man becomes capable of heinous crimes in both high places and low. It is this capability of the human psyche to build a barrier between the mind and the heart that makes cruelty so prevalent, and permits even intelligent and psychologically sound people to follow orders obediently to inflict severe pain and suffering on others.

There may actually be a "death instinct" which prevents unnecessary suffering, and which involves the cessation of all aggression and a withdrawal of the life force. Thus, animals held unhappily in captivity will die regardless of how well their physical needs are met.

This is a common occurrence in humans as well. Infant children raised in institutions and given food and shelter but not love die from a wasting disease called marasmus. It is also well documented that men often die shortly after retirement, and senior citizens after the death of a beloved mate, when life no longer seems to have any meaning.

Learned Helplessness and Depression

There is still another response to perceived danger which animals exhibit, with parallels for humans. When an animal cannot run from the threat and cannot fight it, another part of its autonomic nervous system, called the parasympathetic nervous system, is activated which may shut down all aggressive responses. In its attempt to minimize the energy of impending attack, or to remain in hiding, an animal assumes a posture of total helplessness by "playing dead."

In recent years the syndrome of "learned helplessness" has been recognized by therapists as a habitual coping mechanism that some people adopt to meet life challenges, and which is a variant of the animal pattern of submission, or depression, in the face of a threat. This observation is consistent with Freud's early theories of depression, which hypothesize that depression is the result of anger turned inward. While a person with a hypersensitive alarm system, developed from frequent physical or emotional abuse, might react constantly to the environment with fear and anger to the point of being labeled as "paranoid," an overly submissive person responds to the same environment with learned helplessness, and experiences chronic depression.

Chapter Eleven

How the Brain Responds to the Environment

The Five Major Areas of the Brain Regulating Aggression and Violence in Humans and Animals

In both animals and humans, the brain works like a giant computer to analyze the environment and to respond with a particular behavioral pattern. One or more of the five senses of perception constantly sends random signals to the brain about the environment. There are some basic components of the computer brain that are routinely brought into operation whenever something new is perceived. (See graph, page 118)

A. The Reticular Activating System (RAS) is situated in the midbrain and brain stem. This is the arousal system that awakens the brain to full alertness.

B. The Amygdala is like a central intelligence station that evaluates the nature of all new incoming stimuli from the environment as to whether these stimuli are friendly or hostile.

C. The Limbic System is a "wishbone" structure

encircling the midbrain. This is the "emotional brain," capable of arousing intense anxiety or fear.

D. The Hypothalamus, a large structure in the center of the brain, is a sensory switchboard that regulates autonomic functions. When flooded with fear, it stimulates the Sympathetic Nervous System throughout the body to increase heart rate, blood pressure, and muscle tension.

E. The Outer Cortex (gray matter) comprises the "reasoning" brain. This is especially true of the frontal cortex, which is highly developed in humans. Walter Hess (1949) received the Nobel Prize for demonstrating that the cortex is almost totally dependent on the hypothalamus for instinctual behavioral responses and functioning. However, in humans the "reasoning brain" has the capacity, when disciplined, to gain mastery over the entire circuitry of the lower centers. For example, it can "order" the amygdala to detect only friendliness, and not threats, coming from the presence of other humans. It can also be trained to remain calm in a seemingly threatening situation by viewing the situation from a higher or more mature perspective. As the widely read book, A Course in Miracles suggests, "You can choose to see love instead of hate." (See diagram page 120.)

How the Brain Responds to the Environment

The following is an example of how the above instinctual centers operate constantly in evaluating people who enter our environment.

A. *The Alerting System* (labeled the Ascending Reticular Activating System) in the brain stem awakens the brain and allows it to focus consciously on selected stimuli. It also acts to decrease the awareness of constant stimuli so that the brain can ignore them. The vast majority of incoming messages to the brain are subliminal, which means they are kept below conscious awareness. For example, let us imagine that you are absorbed in reading a newspaper on a park bench, when the voice and presence of an approaching stranger startles you. The alerting center brings you to full consciousness and sends a message to a center in the brain called the...

B. *Amygdala,* which scans the memory patterns of the brain and decides whether this stranger is friend or foe, or someone intending a possibly dangerous violation of your personal space. The amygdala is responsible for setting off a defensive alarm to the...

C. *Limbic System,* which is the emotional circuitry of the brain. It triggers the emotional experience of agitation, hostility, and fear, while arousing the. . .

D. *Hypothalamus,* which chooses a pattern of defensive response, one that is either menacing or submissive. Let us assume that the approaching stranger is a police officer, whose reason for approaching you is unknown. In this instance, the brain will most likely choose to activate the submissive response pattern. Your facial muscles flatten and your eyes help promote the appearance of confused passivity. Your lips may crease slightly into a tight, respectful smile. The alarm system keeps firing because the officer's face has a frown and a stare ("attack" mode) and he appears about to say something that you may not want to hear. So the sympathetic nervous system now increases your heart rate, breathing rate, and muscle tension. The experience is as if someone gave you a shot of adrenaline.

The police officer explains somewhat bruskly that you are parked in a VIP's reserved space and that you must move your car. You jump to oblige. As you drive away the arousal mechanism begins to subside. It may take several minutes for your pulse to return to normal, especially if the officer's demeanor was curt and the tone of his voice reprimanding.

It is from this point that humans differ from animals in that humans have the mental capacity to replay the experience over and over. Resentment may build up as you consider that the officer's manner was disrespectful. An inner dialogue may continue long after the incident. A part of you might be embarrassed for not realizing you were parked in a restricted area. Another part might briefly consider suing the city for "over-restricting access to land that should be open to the public." Finally, you may release some of your pent-up anger at yourself for having behaved toward the officer in an overly-submissive way, by fantasizing your telling him to "Go to hell"—next time.

Because of our advanced intellects, we cannot let go of the little hurts and frustrations of the day but rather allow them to fester in our minds, maintaining us in a more or less constant state of emotional upset.

I once watched a puppy sniffing about on the lawn. Apparently he discovered some cookies or other edible morsels tossed there, because his activity took on an appearance of excitement. A larger dog, passing by, took notice and with a menacing growl took over the smaller dog's find. The smaller dog, with a "Yipe!" surrendered his spot, and without much further ado proceeded to sniff about in an area some ten feet distant in search of another find.

How differently this would be handled by a human! There would likely be a mental rehearsing of the scene for days or weeks, with attempts to seek recourse, legal or otherwise, for revenge. Mental rehashing of situations perceived as insulting, humiliating, or degrading can evoke physiologic responses in the body equal to the original insult, and can result, when all recourse is blocked, in clinical depression.

Chronic Stress Syndrome

The fight-or-flight response triggered by stress causes the release of glucocorticoids. These steroid hormones signal the body to increase blood pressure, heart rate, blood sugar and the flow of blood to the muscles. In the animal kingdom this state of high arousal provides a temporary burst of energy to overcome attack or flee from danger. The body cannot tolerate prolonged periods of such high tension without suffering slow damage to the arteries and organs of the body and, according to recent research, direct damage to the brain cells as well.

This is a common cause of disease and death in our country today. When there is nothing tangible to fight, the environment itself becomes the challenge. This situation results in a constant high level of arousal and stress in the struggle for survival in a complex and highly competitive society. The term "Chronic Stress Syndrome" is gaining acceptance to describe a variety of physical and mental symptoms commonly seen in our medical outpatient clinics. Evidence to indicate that major depression may be one end-point of chronic stress is the finding of adrenal gland enlargement in a significant number of people who suffer from depression.

Stress is now the most common cause of visits to physicians and psychiatrists. Stress is not caused so much by hard work as by negative emotions that fester unresolved in our bodies and accumulates over time. Most employees complain to me about their supervisors or co-workers more than they do about the job itself. No one can hold feelings of anger, jealousy, resentment or worry without eventually have indigestion, heart trouble, headaches, or various abdominal pains.

The first sign of danger is almost always a change in normal sleep patterns. A troubled mind either cannot be shut down or awakens suddenly, fully alert, around four o'clock in the morning and can't go back to sleep. Gradually the adrenal glands, the two small organs that sit on top of each kidney and secrete hormones to combat stress, begin to break down. This breakdown results in a feeling of tiredness, irritability, and impatience, feelings that make these stressed individuals increasingly more difficult to deal with. Blood tests might show a borderline low thyroid level, but taking thyroid only has the effect of whipping a tired horse.

In a predictable sequence over the next several weeks or months, the person suffers increased depression, frustration, inability to concentrate, and sometimes daily anxiety attacks. A stressed individual may try to get more energy by eating more food, especially sweets and salty junk foods, and by drinking caffeinated beverages, but such actions only worsen the condition.

They then begin a series of visits to medical clinics where they receive prescriptions or sleeping pills, tranquilizers, pain pills, blood pressure medication, and antidepressants, all of which seem to help temporarily, while the deterioration of their identity and self-confidence continues. By the time they come to see me, they are convinced that they have a serious psychological distrubance. The best treatment is two weeks of total rest and sleep. But even this approach offers only temporary relief if they are afraid to make the major changes needed in their work or personal relationships.

Unfortunately we live in a society where empathy and support are often replaced with blame, criticism, and personal invalidation, even in the home. Why should life be so difficult? Mainly because there are so few models for relating, communicating, and for solving common problems of living in a complex world. Children yearn for a "User's Manual" for the understanding of themselves, their bodies, and their emotions. Instead they are forced-fed a school curriculum that has no relationship to their real needs, and which offers them no real sense of a personal identity.

When people believe that they cannot influence stressful events so that they are no longer in control of their lives, the body lowers its immune response. This may be a clue as to why depression and a sense of helplessness are associated with cancer. In my opinion it is this, and not aggression as proposed by Freud, that represents the true death instinct in animals and man. The lack of supportive relationships, close family

ties, and a strong sense of community is another contributing factor to early death by heart attacks in men,
and depression in women.

When there is an actual target to fight, an outlet
for aggressive energies, there is concurrent release of
tension, replaced by a sense of purpose and significance.
During World War II the incidence of murder, suicide,
and other forms of violence was significantly lower than
today. When there is no external outlet for frustration,
scapegoats are commonly targeted within a society or
family circle to take the blame for frustration, failure,
and feelings of helplessness. Who can deny that many
targets were pre-selected prior to the outbreak of violence in Los Angeles following the Rodney King jury
verdict in May of 1992?

Under any situation of perceived threat or danger
which, in humans, may be experienced as a sense of
being overwhelmed by a seemingly unending number
of problems, tasks, obstacles, and loss of control over
one's own life, the body becomes charged with emotions ranging from anxiety and fear to anger. This
emotional charge is accompanied by the release of
adrenaline and other hormones that brings the body to
a high level of alertness, tension, and reactivity. The
heart races and shunts blood to the muscular system in
preparation for attack.

Animals normally have their alarm systems activated
for relatively brief periods and only in response to immediate threat. At other times they are generally at rest,
operating within a relatively safe and nurturing environment. Humans, however, feel constantly challenged
by their environment, living in crowded cities, alienated

from one another, where the environment can become unpredictably dangerous at any moment.

Even at home the environment may not be consistently safe, nurturing, and emotionally or physically predictable. Thus, the average person lives constantly in a hostile environment, struggling with inner and outer feelings of alienation. Simultaneously this person experiences increased pressure and expectation for performance and competition for survival.

In the animal kingdom there is a relatively rapid resolution of this high tension state through a climactic encounter or a successful flight. However, in humans the body may be maintained in a relative state of tension for extended periods of time. In fact, this continued tension is becoming more commonly a part of the human condition.

Chronic stress leads to premature breakdown of the physical body, and the most common cause for rising medical costs today. It can result in chronic fatigue and depression. It may be experienced as an inner "powder keg," ready to explode and, especially in males, may result in the anger-to-violence syndrome described in the next chapter.

I can remember my amazement when I heard a retired member of the Green Berets, a highly trained special forces group in the Vietnam War, who frequently engaged in extremely dangerous operations behind enemy lines, state in a television interview that he found much more stressful the day-to-day frustrations and challenges of living in a major city. He explained that during wartime his forays into enemy territory were dangerous but exhilarating, and left him with a sense of a completed mission. And there was always sufficient time allowed after each operation for rest and full recovery before the next. Since he returned home, "the stress level never recedes." Much worse is the build-up of tension and the feeling of helplessness associated with facing an overwhelming accumulation of little problems that don't go away. Like termites they slowly weaken and destroy the infrastructure of the body and the mind.

The important understanding here is that the aggressive mode is rarely stressful. It certainly can be strenuous, but can still be categorized as recreation. When you feel in charge and in control, and experience a sense of excitement rather than fear, there is relatively little build-up of tension. This is an active mode that is compatible with a sense of health and well-being.

Stress results from the defensive mode, the fight-or-flight mode, and especially when you can't run and can't fight. The now familiar Type-A personality who dies of a heart attack in his early fifties is constantly in the defensive mode. He is angrily and impatiently battling other people, fighting against time, and in conflict with himself.

The "normal" stress of day-to-day living has resulted in an expensive overutilization of a medical system that can offer little help, without fundamental psychological and environmental changes in the daily lifestyle of the patient. Doctors can only temporarily postpone the inevitable and minimize symptoms with blood pressure medication, pain killers, and tranquilizers. In addition, escapism, through self-medication with alcohol and illegal street drugs, is pushing our complicated system of law enforcement to its limits.

The graphs on the following pages compare the normal stress patterns of animals in their natural habitat with that of a human being trying to survive in a stressful and competitive environment .

With human behavior, even the relatively normal pace of living in the big city of a technological society can lead to a progressive increase in the state of tension, over time, resulting in high blood pressure, headaches, insomnia, chronic irritability, and other psychosomatic illnesses and even death. The Japanese have a world for it: "Karoshi"—death from overwork. Tens of thousands of Japanese men are dying prematurely from heart attacks and strokes each year due to the competitive pressures inflicted on them for advancement. Attorney Hiroshi Kawahito, head of the National Defense Council for Victims of Karoshi, claims that the health of over ten million Japanese men who work 58-hour weeks without vacations or holidays is being sacrificed to the Japanese work ethic.

(See graph on page 119.)

The way the body was meant to cope with stress, as in the animal kingdom is that each challenge is handled to completion before the next, without a residual build-up of tension. In animals there is a natural, rapid restoration of physiologic mechanisms to normal resting levels between crises. (See graph on page 120)

The Five Major Areas of the Brain Regulating Aggression and Violence in Humans and Animals

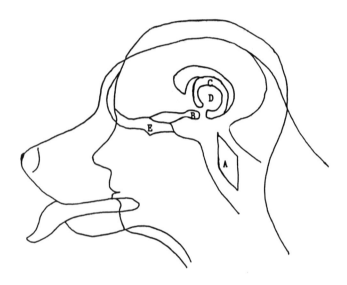

A. Reticular Activating System
B. Amygdala
C. Limbic System
D. Hypothalamus/Thalmus
E. Dog Olfactory Bulb Note: A major difference between dog and human is the dog's much larger ofactory bulb, which helps the animal to evaluate its environment by smell.

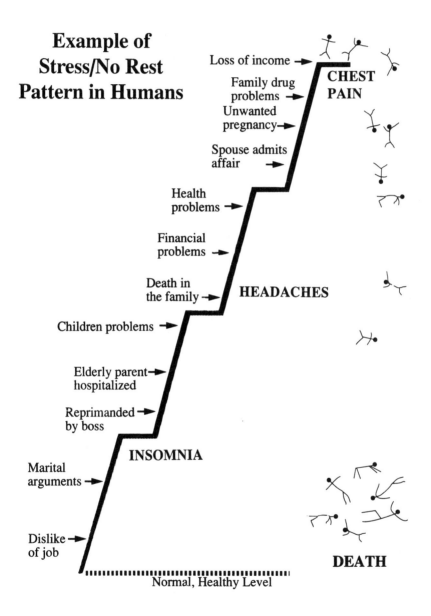

Example of Stress/No Rest Pattern in Humans

Loss of income →

CHEST PAIN

Family drug problems →

Unwanted pregnancy →

Spouse admits affair →

Health problems →

Financial problems →

Death in the family →

HEADACHES

Children problems →

Elderly parent hospitalized →

Reprimanded by boss →

INSOMNIA

Marital arguments →

Dislike of job →

DEATH

Normal, Healthy Level

Stress/Rest Pattern
in the Animal Kingdom

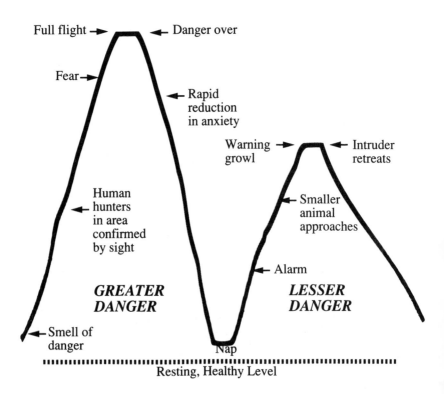

Full flight → ← Danger over

Fear →

← Rapid
reduction
in anxiety

Warning → ← Intruder
growl   retreats

← Human
hunters
in area
confirmed
by sight

← Smaller
animal
approaches

← Alarm

*GREATER
DANGER*

*LESSER
DANGER*

← Smell of
danger

Nap

Resting, Healthy Level

"Going Off"
Anger-To-Violence
Syndrome

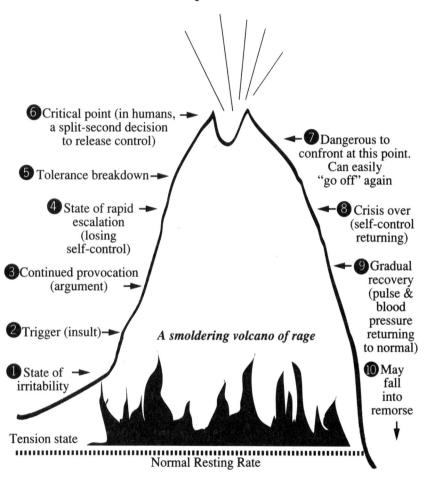

6 Critical point (in humans, → a split-second decision to release control)

5 Tolerance breakdown →

4 State of rapid → escalation (losing self-control)

3 Continued provocation (argument) →

2 Trigger (insult) →

1 State of → irritability

A smoldering volcano of rage

7 Dangerous to ← confront at this point. Can easily "go off" again

← **8** Crisis over (self-control returning)

← **9** Gradual recovery (pulse & blood pressure returning to normal)

10 May fall into remorse ↓

Tension state

Normal Resting Rate

Chapter Twelve

Assessing Violence Potential

Violence potential differs in everyone and is dependent on a number of factors including genetic temperament and personality traits, early childhood traumas, exposure to modeling of violence in the home or in the community, and current environmental stress. Still, after careful consideration of all of these factors the best predictor of violence is a previous history of violence. This is because, in humans, violence involves an inner decision to allow an emotionally irrational, instinctive survival mechanism to take control of the body. Each time a person gives himself permission to act instinctively in a violent manner, his mental discipline against future acts of violence becomes weaker.

In general, deprivation of social contact, coupled with deficits in communication skills, results in the highest potential for violence. The profile of an individual who is prone to violence includes: a pervasive sense of inadequacy, a paranoid orientation toward the environment, and an extreme sensitivity to criticism, rejection, and humiliation. However, this profile does not always fit the increasing number of young adults today who are convicted of senseless violence as a result of environmental and peer pressure.

Violence Is a Learned Behavior

In recent years the view that violence is a learned form of social behavior has gained wider acceptance. Today, violence is indirectly promoted by the media as an unavoidable component of aggression and as an acceptable option to solve a variety of problems. Aggressive behavior is commonly linked to a positive masculine self-image. Aggression is rewarded in sports, glorified by war, and materially lucrative through crime.

Violence, when portrayed on television and in movie scenes that evoke fear and terror, arouses a stimulating adrenal response, primarily in men, where often there is an arousal of sexual stimulation as well. Many of the most popular movies consist of the basic theme of a hero or heroine being thrown back upon basic survival instincts through attack by alien or evil forces. The problem is then handled through raw counter-violence until the enemy is destroyed, revenge is complete, and security is restored.

The world of the entertainment media is portrayed as consisting largely of selfish, power-hungry, unconscionable men and women against whom there are no options other than to kill or be killed. The more humane traits of compassion, receptivity and trust are not only seen as ineffective, but after initially portrayed by the hero or heroine, they are later changed by the realization that counter-violence is the only realistic option for survival.

Learning theory very definitely implicates the movie industry and the mass media as provocateurs of violence. Research with children and adults clearly shows that viewing violence increases the drive to engage in violent acts.

Probably the major factor contributing to the current increase of violence in this country is the combination of environmentally induced frustration coupled with increasing exposure to violent models in the home, in the streets, and on the television screen. Research over the past 25 years shows that there is a definite correlation between aggressive behavior in children and exposure to televised violence, and that the effect accumulates over time. This effect is three-fold:

1. An identification with a hero who resorts to violence and who glorifies violence as a way of extracting justice.

2. A decrease in the restraint against using violence as an option.

3. A progressive desensitization to the pain and suffering of others.

Stress-Related Violence

The environment provided by our largest cities is filled with stress-inducing factors that include pollution (odor, smog, irritants), a high noise level, and crowding. All of these factors are known to have profound deleterious effects on animals held in captivity. Social frustrations due to unemployment, inability to cope with competition, harassment, provocation among ethnic groups, and poor self-concept—all contribute to a feeling of social alienation in our adolescent population most responsible for violent crimes.

However, the resort to violence is still based on learned behavior. In most people, frustration leads to depression. The triad of frustration-depression-anger underlies the growing level of stress in our general population and makes us high users of tranquilizers, anti-depressants, and expensive medical services for stress-related illness. A high level of frustration leads to the seeking of non-specific targets for a release of tension. The high level of tension under which the average person operates can be seen by the level of impatience and intolerance seen on our freeways.

The Anger-to-Violence Syndrome

The anger-to-violence syndrome describes a relatively rapid series of events in which an apparently stable situation becomes suddenly volatile, and a seemingly minor encounter escalates to violence. Sometimes the tightly coiled spring of anger is released by a relatively mild trigger and, after the release, there may be guilt and remorse.

There is a characteristic curve to this anger-to-violence syndrome seen especially in many wife-beaters, child-beaters, and disturbed adolescents. The violence may not be premeditated. However, the individual is predisposed to a low stress tolerance by prior build-up of tension over the previous days or months, and may be "self-medicating" with alcohol or drugs, a practice that only increases his tendency to "explode."

Anger-to-Violence Stages

(See graph, "Going Off," p. 121)

1. A stressed individual has his alarm system on high, which results in a state of mild paranoia. He gives off warning signals by acting irritable or moody. His earlier attempt to calm his nerves with a couple of beers only makes the situation worse by lessening his restraint and self-control.

2. A triggering event, usually in the form of criticism, angry retort, or even a non-verbal gesture portraying disgust or rejection pushes a "button" (an old, unhealed wound from the past).

3. He reacts defensively for a fleeting moment, then suddenly experiences his blood rushing to his head. He counter-attacks angrily, like a cornered animal.

4. His attack is met with a threat, an argument or, even worse, by kidding or mockery from bystanders who are unaware of his now brittle condition.

5. He has reached, in his own mind, the absolute limit of what he can tolerate in terms of abuse and humiliation.

6. This brings him to a critical point where he has only a split second to shut down the whole system and depart from the situation, or to allow his instinctive survival mechanism to take over. His heart is pounding from adrenaline. His stomach is gripped in a

knot. Rage obliterates his fear. The beer he drank now makes it impossible to maintain control.

7. His body erupts into a flurry of violent movements, with the intent of doing as much harm as possible with whatever means or weapons are available to him.

8. He is now legally and clinically in a state of "temporary insanity." Bystanders who attempt to restrain him are also met with the full force of his fury. (Police who attempt to break up a domestic quarrel at this point are at high risk of becoming the target of a lethal attack.)

9. The release of rage through exhaustive discharge gradually restores his rational thinking processes. With this discharge comes a slow comprehension and re-evaluation of his behavior.

10. This comprehension may result in guilt and an attempt to justify the attack to others, i.e., "I was driven to it," or to extreme remorse and depression. Adolescents may have to be watched for suicidal behavior following an impulsive act of violence.

The above scenario is characteristic of that which results in wife-beating. Some husbands may plead with their wives the next day, "Please forgive me, I didn't meant it. Please don't leave me," while the majority will go into denial and try to pretend that it never happened.

I have worked with couples in marriage counseling in which the husband reaches level six (diagram) and, sensing his loss of self-control, will attempt to leave the house. His wife, however, suffering from abandonment fears, blocks his exit, pleading to "talk it over." This, more often than not, results in her becoming the object of assaultive behavior.

Assess Your Own Violence Potential

For many years I have been impressed with how simple mental exercises utilizing visual imagery can uncover feelings that are hidden deep beneath the surface of the mind.

Try the following exercise. Close your eyes after each paragraph and the questions that follow to see what image comes up.

Exercise:

1. Visualize yourself taking a pleasant walk in an area that reminds you of the place where you were raised. Don't try to actively remember, just accept whatever scene comes to mind.

2. You take a turn in the road and you notice a short distance ahead of you a house which has a familiar look to it. The house has two stories and a basement. You notice as you approach that the front door has been left open. You are curious about who lives here and innocently you peek in to chat with the owner. No one is at home.

3. You find yourself checking out the first floor to see what kind of person lives here. Are the rooms small or spacious? Is it dark and stuffy or airy and uncluttered? But what you are really looking for is a door that leads down to the basement.

4. You find the door to the basement. What is down there in the basement is a wild and ferocious animal. However, you are in no danger because the animal is heavily chained. You cautiously walk down the dark steps and find the light switch and there it is! What do you see? What is it doing?

5. Ask yourself: Would it be safe to untie this animal and release it on the streets?

6. Once you see the animal you can notice that it has a different reaction to different people that you know. For example see how differently it would react if you brought your mother and then your father down to see it. Try your boss or spouse or a brother or sister. With one it may become more vicious, with another it might snarl quietly or even cower.

7. Ask yourself: What has made this animal so angry (or frightened)? What would it take to civilize it—to make it into a pet? You might try to visualize yourself becoming the animal in order to get in touch with its feelings.

Interpretation

The animal represents your source of power which was not accepted and from which you yourself may have become alienated and you keep it hidden down deep in your belly.

It is not unusual for a woman with a very sweet personality to see a vicious raging dragon. One woman, for example, who always appeared very timid, saw a raging gorilla which was so deranged that the only option was to shoot it and kill it.

Interestingly, many abused women, and especially those caught up on the servitude trap, often have a cowering or submissive animal for which even the thought of anger is never an option.

In general, the average person relates to others outside of the home setting with a veneer of congeniality. But if sufficiently provoked, this person may give permission to unleash the animal and attack the provocateur with justified violence. Unfortunately this often occurs in the home setting and results in wife-beating or worse. It is as if a different personality temporarily possesses the person, after which they feel embarrassment or remorse or else go into denial, or blame another person for drawing them into a rage. It is in fact a state of temporary insanity.

The important point, however, is that permission to unleash the animal and its subsequent pattern of releasing rage is learned behavior and soon becomes highly predictable because of its repetitive nature.

And again, the adrenaline rush and feeling of power associated with releasing the beast within is highly addictive and its release is greatly enhanced by drugs such as alcohol, PCP, and cocaine.

Chapter Thirteen

The Distinction Between Aggressive and Violent Behavior

To understand the causes of and cures for violence, we must understand the difference between aggression and violence. All aggression does not lead to violence. Even when aggression results in death, this aggression is quantitatively and qualitatively different from the killing that is labeled as violence.

The innate mechanisms governing aggressive behavior and those that promote violence have some important and distinct differences in the mammalian and human brain. The aggressive center is periodically and spontaneously activated both for attack and for play. This center is not motivated either by anger or by fear, but by a hunting instinct for food, and by a natural need for physical expression and interaction. It is often associated with a feeling of exhilaration ("adrenal rush"), but feeling rarely results in an excessive use of force or an intent to cause unnecessary suffering.

Every society offers acceptable outlets for aggression, and its expression may be rewarded with money or praise when it is accompanied by a demonstration of skill or courage. Special conditions are always placed on it, along with the expectation that its execution will be disciplined and controlled. Again, this aggression may or may not involve killing, but in all cases society maintains a prohibition against the use of excessive force.

Socially Condoned Aggression

A. All sporting events (regulated by detailed rules)
B. Hunting (in season)
C. Bull-fighting (within an arena)
D. Animal slaughter (for food)
E. The death penalty (by jury)
F. Military killing (when ordered)
G. Felony killing (by police when necessary)
H. Child spanking (if unemotional)
I. Animal killing (at specified pounds or abattoirs)

Needless to say, all of the above are occasionally questioned by humane and special interest groups as to their appropriateness. In any event, excessive force is always denounced. Even when achieving a military objective, such as in the Gulf War, the possible misuse of excessive force is still being debated. Aggression involving undue pain and suffering is also unacceptable. Hence, cock fighting is declared illegal in this country. The initial protest against the Vietnam War was not motivated by its high cost in money or by loss of military personnel, nor by its dubious political value to this country, but by the leadership's mentality that kept score by "kill ratio." The earliest protesters carried placards saying, "Stop the killing!"

Even the asocial or criminal use of aggression is also characteristically unemotional and concerned more with "precision" than with bloodletting. We may label such killing "cold-blooded murder" because the associated emotions are no different than that of a hunter in killing a deer. Examples include premeditated murder for personal gain by relatively intelligent and successful people, not unlike the villains characterized in the popular detective "Columbo" television series. A hitman for the "mob" was once interviewed on television with a mask over his face. Rather than remorse, he expressed pride in his profession.

Violence, on the contrary, almost always involves an excessive use of force, is motivated by fear and rage, and relishes the eliciting of pain and suffering. Violence is provoked by an activation of the fight-or-flight survival center in the brain as diagrammed earlier. Aggression is an expression of the attack mode from a position of relative strength, while violence is the endpoint of the brain's defensive mechanisms against a perceived threat to the integrity of the self-system.

Aggressive behavior involves whatever is considered a necessary use of force to coerce, control, or kill another living thing. It is self-motivated and uses only the force needed to reach its goal, which is some type of material gain or sense of achievement. In the case of a dog, it barks excitedly when on the hunt or when chasing a cat up a tree. On the other hand, when the same dog is cornered and threatened, it does not bark. Rather, it gives a warning growl and snarls, and will become violent if provoked beyond this point.

Aggressive behavior in humans is made more acceptable by depersonalizing the victim. For example, going hunting or fishing usually elicits no more remorse than climbing a hill to pick wild berries. On the other hand, the movie *Bambi* personalized a mother doe, thus depicting her murder as a tragic act of violence.

In acts of aggression the object has a relatively impersonal identity, whereas with violence the victim has a very real identity, if often a symbolic one, and is seen as having a source of power that was wrongly used to seduce, threaten or harm the attacker who is now seeking vengeance.

Violence, by the definition given in this book, in contrast to aggression, is always motivated by defensive fear and rage. It most often results from a slow build-up of rage due to repeated provocation or to continual nursing of old hurts and wounds, accompanied by pleasurable fantasies of a particular act of violence against a specific target. In either case there is a build-up of rage to a point where rational objectivity is lost and a sense of justification prevails over normal constraints. Finally, a level of tolerance breakdown occurs in which inner permission, accompanied by a sense of righteous conviction, allows the tightly coiled spring of emotional rage to release in a frenzy of unrestrained discharge, which mimics closely the premeditated fantasy.

In most cases the violence is not lethal and consists only of a verbal discharge in which the tongue is used as a sword to cut deeply into the emotional belly of a perceived aggressor. This type of verbal violence is unfortunately common in the home environment, and can have devastating consequences for children, whether or not they are the primary target. It creates deep emotional wounds that fester fantasies of their own. Thus murder within one's own circle of family and acquaintances remains the major cause of homicide in this country.

To understand more simply how we all make the decision for or against violence almost daily, consider a situation in which you are repeatedly belittled by your boss in front of other workers. The process may begin inside you with the thought, "One of these days I'm going to let him have it back." This thought starts a mental counting system that accumulates tension as it records and magnifies each new hurt until your own personal tolerance breakdown point is reached and suddenly, for a seemingly minor harassment, you unleash your well-rehearsed verbal counter-attack on your unsuspecting and startled boss.

The threat of dire consequences will raise a person's tolerance breakdown threshold level, but sometimes this threat only postpones the inevitable, because at any tolerance breakdown level, by definition, the consequences have lost their meaning. This is why the perpetrators of violent crimes are often willing to sacrifice their own lives in an act of vengeance, or may make little initial attempt to cover up or deny what they have done, so strong lingers the irate sense of self-justification. This is why punishment is not a significant deterrent to violence.

Violent behavior is always defensive behavior in the eyes of the perpetrator. It is seen as retaliation for a past or current insult, injustice, or humiliation. Anger is the natural biological and emotional response to fear, helplessness, humiliation or rejection. Rejection creates what psychiatrists call a "narcissistic injury." This feeling of injury can often result in violence or the threat of violence by ex-husbands and rejected lovers.

The fantasy of "teaching someone a well-deserved,

painful lesson," can provide a temporary sense of satisfaction when no other avenues are open to express
anger or to redress a wrong. However, every fantasy
of violence, each time it is recreated in the mind, carries an increasing likelihood of being acted out. When
pushed to the tolerance breakdown point, the will is
forced to make a critical decision of whether to act out
in violent rage, to crumble into fearful surrender, or to
withdraw into deep depression. The decision depends
on the options open in terms of weapons and support
available, and the direction that previous fantasies have
taken around this situation.

A good general rule is: never provoke with a dare,
or give an ultimatum to a man engaged in the process
of committing a violent act. A number of instances have
been reported in the newspapers, of situations in which
a man is holding his wife, children or other people as
hostages with the threat to kill them. The fact that he
has delayed in following through with the ultimate act
suggests that a small part of his reasoning mind still
maintains some flicker of tenuous control or doubt. This
possibility needs to be supported in every way, including sympathetic communication. Time, itself, is a major
factor on the side of the reasoning mind. To prematurely force an ultimatum upon this man is almost
guaranteed to precipitate the fulfillment of the violent act.

Consent of the will in fantasy is consent of the will
in action, given the right set of circumstances. Consequences are important only if they stop the initial train
of fantasy. Violence can be reduced only when the educational system teaches young children alternative options
for expression and for coping with stress. All behavior
has a preceding history that gives clues to its motives,

as well as a follow-up sequel that either promotes or diminishes the likelihood of the behavior being repeated.

Experience has shown that administering punishment during or after a given act may increase the apprehension or guilt experienced when repeating the behavior, but does not significantly lessen its occurrence. The caveat must come before the behavior. There must be a prohibition at the point in which thinking about the behavior begins. To paraphrase the Bible: To sin in the mind is only a short step from sinning in the flesh. The only reliable deterrent to any behavior is to make it unthinkable. As an example, son-mother rape is unthinkable, and consequently, a rare event.

There is rarely an act of violence that has not been fantasized and rehearsed in the mind, many times before its final execution. Non-violence must be taught to young children at every level. Acts of violence must be proscribed as unthinkable. Unfortunately we have a television media that glorifies violence and makes what was unthinkable in my generation fashionable in the present one. I dread the day when daring writers begin to challenge the taboo against mother rape.

Thus violence is best eliminated by prevention. This prevention must begin with a stabilization of the family unit and be followed by a renovation of our educational system, with a major focus on non-technological communication skills. Opportunities for personal growth, for material gain, and for self-esteem through healthy aggressive channels must be taught and made generally available. Leadership training is important, also. Strong leadership may organize mass demonstrations, but with a control that keeps violence in check.

Again, the importance of making a distinction between violence and aggression is that each defines
distinctly separate behaviors. Violence is motivated by
fear, helplessness, and a sense of impotence. Its goal is
punishment and revenge for a prior defeat, and never
serves its perpetrator any useful, tangible gain. Violence
is the last resort of failed aggression such as the burn-
ing of the oil wells in Kuwait, and the Nazi holocaust
in World War II. The time that any leadership or regime must resort to violence to maintain its power base
is a sign that its end is inevitable.

The outbreak of violence, which results from a tolerance breakdown within a particularly victimized
segment of the population, is only a warning signal
that will not spread further if properly addressed, instead of responded to with counter-violence. Punishment
only inflames violence which, by definition, has already
lost its rational fear of consequences.

Violence, once begun, quickly reaches an exhaustion
phase, at which point it may be significantly diminished by concessions. But these concessions must lead
to some form of meaningful empowerment. Again, grass
roots leadership must be encouraged, not imprisoned.
Leadership may result in aggression, but aggression is
amenable to rules. The regime that is too inflexible to
handle violence in this way will eventually crumble.

Aggression is the controlled use of power for personal gain. Aggression conforms to a consistent set of
rules. Considerable aggression is tolerated, even admired,
in our society as long as it remains disciplined from
overstepping its boundaries into violence. Aggression by
corporations or organized crime may be altruistic, selfish, hedonistic or asocial, but is still influenced by the

norms and regulations of the greater society. It may involve the constant testing of every rule, and a repeated attempt to expand existing boundaries and limits, but it never directly attacks the system itself, with which it enjoys a parasitic relationship.

Aggression by the established bases of power in our society, which include our large corporations, has become increasingly self-serving and relatively indifferent to the health of the planet and to the people left homeless by their bulldozer policies. Contrary to the political attitude maintained over the past twelve years, an attitude that has brought our country to the brink of moral and financial ruin, it is definitely the duty of government to protect the safety and the rights of its people by maintaining strong regulatory powers over every activity that affects the health, wealth, and the environment of the people. It requires strong and courageous political leadership to maintain the type of discipline and balance of all business enterprises which will ultimately serve the best interests of each of them.

The burden of responsibility rests on our educational system, which must begin with the young in inculcating ethical and spiritual values, a sense of moral conscience, and the attitude of cooperation and service into the fabric of their self-concept. However, these are the same schools that have failed our society in ignoring the real developmental needs of our children, who now pass through their critical stages of growth with a lack of self-discipline, a disrespect for authority, and a "me-first" attitude.

Organized crime, like large a corporation, has its own leadership, organization, rules, and discipline. Both live symbiotically within the system, and except for an occasional investigation and indictment, remain relatively untouched, as long as they refrain from violence that arouses public outcry, and especially if they do not directly attack the system. Both are subject to the influence of legislation, legal rulings, public attitudes regarding their products, and the threat of specific penalties.

Aggressive behavior by large corporations, which results in the denuding of our rain forests, the contamination of our drinking water and the pollution of our atmosphere, is a far more serious problem than the violent behavior of victimized minority groups protesting against inequality. Once a disadvantaged group attains a strong leader and assumes an organized and planned direction toward empowerment, its behavior can be labeled as aggression. But what's the fear? History has shown that the fears of the establishment are always unfounded. Killing a leader only delays the inevitable and increases potential for violence.

CHART OF CHARACTERISTIC DIFFERENCES

	AGGRESSION	VIOLENCE
Personality Type:	Strong	Unstable
Motive:	Expression of Power	Perceived Injustice
Goal:	Personal Gain	Revenge
Emotion Before:	Excitement	Rage
Emotion After:	Exhilaration	Release of Tension
Brain Mechanism:	Attack	Defense
Ego State:	Controlled	Dyscontrol
Attitude to Target:	Indifference	Obsessed
Reaction to Consequences	Concerned	Indifferent

AGGRESSION OR VIOLENCE
Q & A

Circle one:

A or V   1.   The Gulf War.

A or V   2.   Deer hunting.

A or V   3.   Parent disciplining a child.

A or V   4.   Man kills a jewelry clerk during an armed robbery. When asked why, he replies, "She didn't follow the rules. " When asked whose rules, he replies, "My rules."

A or V   5.   A homeless girl kills another homeless girl in order to take her sweater.

A or V   6.   Dan White kills Mayor Moscone after the Mayor refuses to reinstate him on the Board of Supervisors.

A or V   7.   Saddam Hussein's torching of the Kuwait oil wells.

A or V   8.   Date rape.

A or V   9.   A man in a wheelchair shoots his wife for threatening to leave him.

A or V   10.   A young man returns to his high school to kill the history teacher who had flunked him.

A or V   11.   A brilliant teenager kills himself after losing a debate competition.

A or V   12.   A mother tells young children playing noisily to keep quiet. They ignore her. After the sixth warning she rushes into their room and spanks them.

A or V   13.   A wife nags her alcoholic husband in front of the children, to stop drinking.

A or V   14.   A high school girl fatally stabs a friend who won the head cheerleader position, over her.

A or V   15. A "hit man" for organized crime, interviewed on TV wearing a mask, says that he feels no guilt for killing.

A or V   16. The Los Angeles Police beating of Rodney King.

Answers

1. Aggression:
It was purportedly the only rational decision left open to protect the rest of the world, and was controlled so that only military targets were hit. However, whether an excessive amount of force was used is still being debated. The importance of this question is that if answered in the affirmative, the action becomes an act of violence, and violence is deplored by the world community.

2. Aggression:
As a sport—without intention to cause unnecessary suffering, and provided rules and regulations are followed regarding season, weapons used, and number of kills allowed.

3. Aggression:
Discipline is an example of positive aggression. This is a two-way gain made possible by mutual respect. The same is true for competitive sports between players who respect each other.

4.   Aggression:
Although not socially condoned, this was an unemotional act for personal gain, by rules which he announced beforehand. He "had a job to do," and no excessive force would be used if everyone "follows the rules." This callous attitude is a throwback to primitive dominant behavior.

5.   Aggression:
An example of how "cold-blooded" aggression devalues life for personal gain. Empathy, respect, and value for life need to be taught at an early age.

6.   Violence:
The motive was revenge upon a specifically selected target with no possible gain for anyone.

7.   Violence:
Revenge for a failed aggression with no perceivable benefit to anyone.

8.   Aggression:
An example of the selfish seeking of pleasure, which has become increasingly more common in young adult males. There is callous disregard for the rights and feelings of the other person, but usually there is no intent to cause suffering, and most likely an unawareness of the actual harm being done. Date rape is the result of an undisciplined mind giving license to a normal instinctive drive upon a target of opportunity. In the past women rarely complained because they believed that they would be held responsible because men are not expected to have any control over their sex drive.

9.   Violence:
An act of revenge for rejection. He justified his action when interviewed later, in jail: "She was killing me by what she was doing."

10. Violence:
Senseless killing for no gain by an emotionally disturbed young man.

11. Violence:
Anger turned against the self for not living up to performance expectations.

12. Violence:
A common example of a parent who does not know how to discipline her children properly. Instead, she lets them push her to her tolerance breakdown point, which brings anger and a feeling of justifiable assault. Punishment is always the last resort of failed discipline. It has its place if unemotional, and if the rules have been made clear beforehand.

13. Violence:
Nagging is a form of belittlement and degradation that serves no useful purpose other than a release of pent-up anger. The wife feels like a victim, helpless and trapped, and wants her husband at least to suffer some guilt. The core problem here is that the wife is being forced to assume the dominant position, which she resents. Similarly, a wife will nag a weak husband in an attempt to make him a man. She feels disillusioned and betrayed by being shackled with a little boy instead of a supportive adult man.

14. Violence:
The Performance Trap has taken on such an emotional charge that, even at the high school level, success or failure is a matter of life or death.

15.   Aggression:
Like a hired mercenary, he was paid to do a job.

16.   Aggression (Violence?):
According to the jury, policemen are licensed to use means of force, including guns and billy clubs, to protect themselves and the public. They are not licensed to use excessive force. The tape appeared to indicate, to the public, that they used excessive force. And so the debate goes on. (At this printing, two of the officers were judged by a federal jury of being guilty of using excessive force.)

Chapter Fourteen

Beyond the Pecking Order

What is a human being, and how do humans differ from the animal kingdom? We can say that we have highly specialized brains, with large frontal lobes and extra convolutions in our gray matter, factors that enable us to engage in abstract thinking and complex reasoning. Perhaps our dilemma is accurately symbolized by the Great Sphinx of Egypt: a spiritual being entrapped in an animal body.

In any event, until we understand more about the nature of our animal body and its built-in patterns of coping and survival, we will continue to be deluded by the notion that our behavior is determined largely by free will.

We are gifted with a mind that can control every facet of our physical body. Yet without a respectful awareness of the innate instincts and drives of the physical body, and without proper training and a disciplined mind, sooner or later the emotional needs, the drive for power, the sexual urge and the survival instincts of the physical body, will ultimately run the mind.

Humans normally have a strong intellectual defensive mechanism, which serves to hold in check

149

instinctive impulses and drives, so that they can behave in a socially acceptable manner. The result, for the average person, is inner conflict and neurosis. Why are animals, who apparently have no such defenses, less troubled and able to behave more humanely to one another in social structures, than do humans? Perhaps it is because animals do not experience an alienation between their inner world and their outer world of nature.

And why don't animals, like most humans, have to expend immense psychic energy in suppressing an inner volcano of rage that threatens constantly to erupt at every provocation? Perhaps if humans within a given family or social system accepted each other unconditionally, as animals accept one another within their social groupings, there would be little need for the defensive functions of the ego and for the constant storing of rage.

Until we accept the inseparable relationship of the physical body to nature, and obey the laws governing all of nature, we cannot prevent the body's breakdown and premature aging despite all of the technological advances of medicine.

As each civilization becomes more complex, it paradoxically becomes more dehumanizing, more stressful, and more out of touch with the natural order or things. Eventually it decays from the center outward, as its core breeds malaise, depression, and violence. This is the problem facing all of our major cities today: the insidious corruption of human values breeding self-alienation and violence. None of this is natural to nature. Rather, it is the result of severing our bond to nature and to the natural flow of the underlying order that sustains life on this planet.

The mind of man has the power to create beautiful edifices, spacious cities, and complex social systems. But lest he be constantly aware of the danger, he too easily becomes entrapped in these structures of his own making. His identity becomes lost in the artificial fabric of a great, creative cultural illusion that now veils him from his true identity and his primordial interdependence with nature.

We live in a materialistic world dominated by the left brain. From a very early age children are taught to exercise their left brains for spelling, math, and the memorization of endless mimeographed pieces of information to the exclusion of their right brains. Yet it is our right brain, the creative and intuitive aspect of our nature, that is by far our greatest asset and the source of every major new discovery.

A balance between the two is needed. Proper use of this balance, under a disciplined mind, yields the greatest fulfillment of our potential. Young children are primarily right-brained, which means that they experience the totality and wholeness of nature without dissecting it. Once they make the shift to the reasoning intellect, they cease to experience the real world, except in terms of what they tell themselves.

Children are naturally attracted to any information which leads to self-discovery. Consciousness has an urge to grow but needs a medium by which to grow. That medium may involve any new experience, conflict, crisis or problem.

Passive information offers no medium for real growth. It is linear, verbal and one-dimensional. Human beings are multidimensional. Learning comes from experience and is primarily nonverbal. Boredom results from a situation in which a person is not a witness to his own growth.

One of the problems with our educational system is that it puts data into the left brain as answers, instead of questions. This not only limits, but obstructs, the creative function of the right brain. It is not so much what schools teach as what they do not teach that makes a tragic waste of the precious opportunity they have to influence positively the minds of young children during their most receptive and impressionable formative years. Schools might better serve society if they would focus on the real lessons that children need to learn:

1. They need to learn to appreciate their growing bodies and to respect their individual differences of color, size, talents, proclivities, and sensitivities.
2. They need to understand their emotions and feelings, learn to articulate their needs and fears, and trust their inner knowing.
3. They need to learn how to ask the right questions instead of being fed answers and labels that take away all the awe and mystery of the life around them.
4. They need to look inward as well as outward, and to explore all the levels at which communication can take place.
5. They need to know their connection to nature, their bond to one another, the grandeur of their being, and the value of their caring.
6. They need to know of their innocence, of the fallibility of adults, and of what is them and what is not them.

7. They must dare to have dreams, to honor the desires of the heart, and to learn the meaning of love at every level.
8. They need to learn about kindness, sharing, responsibility, and self-discipline as the foundation for maturity and success as adults in the world.

Perhaps, if there were one word to describe what is needed most in the world today and which is lacking at the level of the family, among the various subgroups in our society, and among the nations of the world, that word would be "communication." Paradoxically, the explosive growth in technological transmission of information around the world has made close, interpersonal communication nearly obsolete.

During the first five years of schooling, children should spend more time learning to communicate with one another than listening to the teacher. Interpersonal communication is the basis for learning. However, now, during the first two years of school, all of the major modes of communication are stifled to the exclusion of technological communication.

My own report cards were always down-graded because of "conduct." I was always "caught whispering," a behavior that was treated as a mortal sin. I wanted to discuss, share, get involved. I must have heard the teacher say, "Mind your own business, Ernest," ten times a day. In retrospect, I was trying to mind my own business. Everyone I can see, touch, or reach with my whisper is my business, part of my world, a brother or sister sharing the life experience.

We are trained to go through life in our own little booths, trying to mind our own business. It makes us paranoid. People who live in an apartment house in a city of a million people are lonely because of this training. A woman is being knifed on the sidewalk in New York City with 35 people watching from their windows, every one of them minding their own business, until she is dead.

Why is everyone so busy? Where are all the people rushing to go? They are afraid that if they stop, they will get in touch with their loneliness. We don't have time to really make contact, to really touch each other, or to fully savor life. Certainly, we are not taught this in school. Life is outside the windows of the dreary rectangular classroom. Finally, the bell rings announcing the end to one more long day of confinement.

Those whose parents want to push them toward success will have precious little time to savor the outdoors because of the added burden of homework. What if a child could be made to study endless hours until he read the entire *Encyclopedia Britannica*? What then? Very few highly successful men would credit their high school or college classes for their success. In any event, six hours per day of linear thinking is sufficient for any child.

As the unit of the family goes, so goes the social structure. Children search for a sense of significance in the eyes of the adults about them, as they reach out for emotional bonding and love. When they see eyes clouded with fear, worry, and indifference, their spark of innocence becomes encapsulated in a protective wall. Something in them begins to die, as anger covers their hurt feelings.

Civilization, with its social constraints and enforced, suppressive learning environments, promotes the progressive dehumanization of children. There is a loss of bonding to nature, and with this, a loss of essential being and worth. Children become out of touch with inner reality at the cost of serving an outer reality. Spiritual values are reduced to empty concepts and religious ritual. They develop a negative emotional state which, like heavy smog, clouds their consciousness with fear, confusion, overwhelm, and apprehension. Behind it all is the heart's aching for spiritual nurturance.

People use street drugs and prescription drugs in large quantities to calm the mind's frantic clamoring for the harmony that only nature knows. In every human being there is inner loneliness and an inner desperate search for something, anything to fill the void left by the loss of essential purpose and being. Once the tie to nature is severed, resonance with the inner and the outer world is lost, and with it an instinctual sense of one's ground of being.

The outer world is seen as an enemy, a competitor, a barrier to the fulfilling of one's inner needs. Attacking or blaming someone out there becomes a way of easing conflict within. Stresses of day-to-day coping create inner conflict, irritability, frustration, and a desire to give up or resort to violence. It is as if something imprisoned inside is crying out for expression, regardless of the consequences. Creating more prisons is not the answer.

Psychiatrists have only recently placed emphasis on exploration of the human qualities of basic goodness and love. The power of love when activated can overcome the forces of hate. Researchers now seriously term love as a nutrient, and compare its role with Iodine and Vitamin C. There is some evidence that love even influences the growth of children's bones. It certainly affects a child's ability to learn in school; it is the foundation of emotional health, the magic wand that lifts the curse of self-dislike.

Perhaps it is important that we learn to get in touch with our own potential for anger, perhaps to avoid hurting others, perhaps to recognize the violent potential of those with whom we work every day, perhaps to be aware of our own triggers that can result in brief lapses of rational thinking, perhaps to have compassion for the actions of those who feel less lovable than we feel.

Anger is not something we must deal with in order to proceed along the business of human social interaction, but rather it is the disease itself, the causes and cure of which deserve our prime attention and focus.

That is why it is so important that we learn to understand the capacity we all have to love, and the power inherent in loving to dissolve anger and fear.

We are human beings in an animal body, and as such are subject to all of the baser emotions common to the animal kingdom. But whereas anger and fear are survival mechanisms to provoke attack or to assist in flight in lower animals, these emotions serve no useful purpose in man. We are unique from all other species in possessing a center of high awareness, intuition, knowing, and will. Then, too, we have an intellect that weighs, judges, and is capable of rational decisions.

Only when we lose sight of the special nature of our being do we regress into helplessness and fear, and then bring senseless suffering to ourselves and to others. The motives of animals are based on survival of the species and the pain/pleasure principle. In humans the prime purpose of all activity is toward freedom to restore to oneself the full awareness of who we are. The pain/pleasure principle only temporarily satisfies the pain, despair, and loneliness created by our deeper memory of separation from whence we came and the yearning for the oneness we once knew. So sense pleasures, physical pleasures, are sought as a desperate measure to try temporarily to satisfy something that can not be satisfied in this way. The yearning, the emptiness, the longing, the loneliness, the incompleteness, the dissatisfaction, are still there behind it all.

Konrad Lorenz, who pointed out the universal existence of an aggressive instinct in the animal kingdom, later acknowledged that "...greater feelings of love and friendship for others may prove incompatible with the expression of overt aggression." Ideally, as we evolve as a people, extreme polarities such as master-slave gradually merge into a brotherhood of equality. This is the inner battle we all must resolve, the struggle between self-serving isolation and cohesive communion with one another.

In the course of an average lifetime each person plays many roles in a variety of relationships with others, including parent-child, husband-wife, teacher-student, and boss-employee. These relationships are held together by our gregarious nature and an innate need to create and sustain a meaningful social bond. Through these experiences we learn something about giving and receiving, the rewards of service, the responsibilities of authority, and the right use of power.

Rollo May stated, "...no human being can exist for long without some sense of his own significance." As humans we must learn the true meaning of power. The misuse of power leads to estrangement and an endless search for significance through control, domination, and violence. The right use of power is for empowerment of others. One's own sense of significance can best be measured by the willingness and the desire to enhance the significance of others.

In the animal kingdom, power is expressed through instinct and emotion. In the spiritual man, power is expressed through reason and love. Fear and competition bred by our current society closes the heart. With the heart closed, man becomes enamored of himself. Then the greater the wisdom, the greater the pride. When the heart is open, the greater the wisdom, the greater the appreciation and awe of the fathomless mystery of life all around us.

Postscript

Reflections upon the Growing Vision of Psychology Toward a Broader Concept of the Human Mind

It is an interesting coincidence that the date of publication of this book coincides with the 30th anniversary of my professional career as a psychiatrist. It is somewhat amazing to me to realize that this time period spans more than one-third of the history of the field of psychiatry as we know it in the Western world. Less than one hundred years ago Freud was ridiculed for proposing that our conscious feelings and behaviors were only like the surface screen on the monitor of a giant computer and orchestrated by hidden programs that were created by childhood experiences now long forgotten. Psychoanalysis, he claimed, was not so much a therapy as a means of accessing the hidden computer files. This view challenged the scientific thinking of his time, a pattern of thinking that had emerged from the "Age of Reason."

The Age of Reason had focused upon the "scientific method" to quantify reality. It assumed that whatever was not seen, and easily verifiable by others did not exist. Perhaps this way of thinking provided the only viable escape from the Dark Ages, when untethered minds created all sorts of hidden and terrifying demons and life was filled with uncertainty and fear. The scientific method developed the left brain at the expense of the right brain, which became harnessed in the interest of preserving some semblance of predictability, sanity and control over the world.

It was in this atmosphere of Newtonian thinking, which

emphasized the principle of the preservation of energy, that Freud attempted to develop a "scientific" working model of the mind. He must be credited with introducing intuitive insights, which expanded the Western world's concept of the mind. He divided mental life into conscious and unconscious, and described the conscious as a thin mantle at the mercy of deep urges and strivings of the unconscious. He described a hidden mechanism that he labeled the "ego," whose function is to maintain a comfortable homeostasis or balance between the inner emotional environment and the outer world over which it had no direct control. Actually, Freud was being far more conservative than he realized when he limited the unconscious mind to the pain-pleasure principle and easily definable instincts.

Freud's brilliant protégé, Karl Jung, became intrigued with the spiritual philosophies of the Far East, especially of India and China, and dramatically expanded Freud's concept of the unconscious, especially in the interpretation of dreams. In dreams Jung saw universal symbols that suggested a hidden network connecting all human beings and creating a consensus reality or myth composed of universal archetypes. In effect, what Jung was trying to propose to Freud was the seemingly outlandish idea that we are all trapped in the same dream and telepathically engaged in a cosmic game not unlike Dungeons and Dragons. This dream he asserted, veils our true identity.

Freud reportedly screamed at Jung, "You are opening the Pandora's box of Eastern mysticism." Jung was stepping too far beyond his own, "scientific" method of neatly categorizing behavior. During one of their heated confrontations Freud, who saw Jung's rebellion against him as a father transference, literally fell into a faint after shouting, "You are trying to kill me."

Yet Jung continued to question, "What is the secret of the whole person?" And as he looked still deeper, he found that there was yet more to discover.

Most psychologists today would agree with the basic premise that at an early age we develop an identity or sense of who we are in relation to the world, and that all of our subsequent behavior evolves from this identity. The task of the psychotherapist is to upgrade this identity dramatically, or risk a repetition of problems that this identity creates.

Helpful advice is almost always useless. We can see this fact more clearly if we consider popular television personalities such as Archie Bunker, Rosanne Arnold, Jackie Gleason, and Lucille Ball in "I Love Lucy." Their problems are essentially variations on the same theme from week to week. It would be senseless, for example, to suggest to Archie Bunker that he take up western dancing in order to socialize more. Every identity operates within a very narrow range. The therapist who focuses only upon problem-solving and assisting an identity to be more comfortable or functional may actually be contributing to that patient's stuckness. Identity, then, is the key that determines the role we play in life and, indeed, the very life we choose to live.

Whenever we block expression in children, we damage their self-image. However, most parents consider their children to be "good" if they remain quiet, suppressing any expression of energy or need so that they are not seen as a nuisance or a burden to the adults around them. Children are taught directly or by innuendo by their parents, by the media, by our educational system, and by our churches that there is more evil than good within them. Even Freud felt that civilization offers a protective veneer over our selfish and destructive inner impulses.

Quite to the contrary, deeper exploration of the mind sees within each of us the powerful and beautiful spirit that cries out for expression. Within every adult I meet I see a lonely child crying for acceptance. People want that glimpse of recognition from others that says, "I see you," which makes them feel "real." Whenever people feel, for even a brief moment, that they are lovable and truly loved they usually break down in tears, as the newly selected Miss America always does.

The social structure of a society determines how to earn a sense of significance through guidelines based on comparison and competition. For those few who are able to win awards and trophies there is a momentary flush of exhilaration that comes with being acknowledged, being loved, and being real. But tomorrow they must begin anew to prove their worth.

I have treated depression in many young students who attend major colleges and universities in the Bay Area. These students complain of a sense of emptiness or longing which I am beginning to recognize as spiritual hunger. Disease, depression, and violence result from our society's denial of the positive, healing, spiritual energies inherent within each individual, and the special gift each has for creative accomplishments.

Children do not grow by having mimeographed information jammed into their heads, but rather from learning how to access the "modem" that they already have within themselves, connected to intuitive "knowing." They need to understand the power of their own minds to create whatever new environment they choose, instead of becoming trapped within the frightening environment created by their parents.

In the past 30 years we have seen the growth of humanistic, existential, and transpersonal psychologies that broaden dramatically the concept of human consciousness. These psychologies view our daily problems and struggles from the context of an ongoing evolutionary process. Transpersonal psychology in particular seeks to address the underling questions behind the human condition:

What is Life?
Who are we?
What is our purpose?
Is there a God?

Abraham Maslow, who is credited by some as being the father of transpersonal psychology, argued eloquently for a stronger emphasis on the psychologically healthy person instead of on psychopathology. In his book *Motivation and*

Personality (1954) he states: "Aggression and destructiveness, for example, are not indigenous to man. He becomes pugnacious and destructive when his inner nature is twisted or denied or frustrated. As soon as the frustration is removed, aggression disappears."

Psychedelic drugs such as LSD have opened a whole new inquiry into extraordinary states of consciousness that had previously been labeled, in patients who described these experiences spontaneously, as psychosis. Dr. Stanislav Grof is probably the world's foremost researcher in doing psychotherapy with psychedelic drugs such as LSD. Through his work, spanning three decades, Grof discovered that higher dimensions of consciousness can be accessed in the average person without the use of pharmacological agents. Rather, these states can be attained through music, rhythmic breathing, and various sensory techniques.

Grof makes use of these techniques in his revolutionary approach to psychotherapy, an approach that he calls Holotropic Therapy. He enumerates in his latest book, *The Adventures of Self-Discovery*, (1988), the vivid experiences described by his patients. These include identification with the entire physical universe, encounters with spirit guides and extraterrestrial beings, and time travel into past-life experiences.

Dr. Grof states that his findings "throw entirely new light on the material from history, comparative religion, and anthropology concerning the ancient mysteries of death and rebirth, rites of passage of various cultures, shamanic procedures of all times, aboriginal healing ceremonies, spiritual practices of various religious and mystical traditions, and other phenomena of great cultural significance."

This past year my good friend, Winafred Lucas, completed her painstakingly edited two-volume work: *Regression Therapy* (Deep Forest Press, 1993), in which she examines the teachings and findings of the world's foremost researchers in the growing field of regression therapy. Just as Stanislav Grof found, these experienced therapists are able, through various relaxation techniques, to access in the majority of their patients states of consciousness that transcend time and space and the paradigm of the material world as we know it.

Dr. Brian Weiss's recent book: *Many Lives Many Masters*, which is about a reincarnation experience in a patient, has become an instant best seller. The book's popularity would have been unlikely had he written it twenty years ago. But it speaks to the growing need by increasing numbers of the population for answers to the meaning and purpose of their lives, a meaning that science and technology do not provide.

Recent years have also revealed an increasing interest and awareness of the spiritual wisdom of the Native American. Hyemeyohsts Storm comments in his book *Seven Arrows* (1972): "According to the Teachers, there is only one thing that all people possess equally. This is their loneliness. No two people on the face of this earth are alike in any one thing except for their loneliness. This is the cause of our Growing, but it is also the cause of our wars. Love, hate, greed and generosity are all rooted within our loneliness, within our desire to be needed and loved."

We are lonely because we do not communicate. And families who try to communicate usually argue. Active listening with focused attention is equated with love. I sometimes get a chuckle from my students at the Rosebridge Graduate School of Integrative Psychology by suggesting that Freud was a genius for reasons other than his discovery of psychoanalysis in that he developed a structure by which, for the first time in the recorded history of the world, you could talk to an intelligent father figure who keeps silent and listens to you with focused attention for an entire fifty minutes.

Karl Jung noted that the psychopathology of the masses is rooted in the psychopathology of the individual. Long before the onset of the Second World War Jung began to notice peculiar mythological motifs that he called "archetypes" in the dreams of his German patients. He described the "Wotun" or "Blond Beast" archetype associated with primitive violence and cruelty. When such symbols occur in a large number of individuals, and are not properly understood and integrated, he claimed, they erupt to the surface en masse, creating a "holocaust," which brings to the conscious mind both the existence of these symbols and the need to deal with them. This phenomenon occurs naturally every generation or so. We must not underestimate these inner forces. Yet Jung warned that a person could not be freed from these archetypal complexes without understanding.

Thus, the salvation of humanity appears dependent upon our willingness to bring to conscious awareness the counterbalancing "spiritual" forces inherent within all of us. These forces include our capacity for integration, harmony, order, and love, especially in our relationships with our fellow human beings.

How do we judge the whole person? Early in my training I had a thought-provoking experience. I was treating a young man who was socially dysfunctional, chronically depressed, and who had never completed high school. He was the product of an unwanted pregnancy and had never known his father. When his mother married and started a family he was essentially discarded and shunted off to various relatives and foster homes.

He lived in San Francisco on a meager Welfare dole and got caught up in casual homosexual relationships, feeling too inadequate to find friendship as a heterosexual. He required medication to reduce his negative obsessive thoughts, which were aimed mainly at himself. Needless to say, his self-image had reached rock bottom. He felt unworthy and apologized for taking my time to speak to him.

However, I was intrigued with his caring disposition, his lack of anger and resentment, and his concern for other people he met who were similarly troubled or homeless. He had a penchant for buying gifts for others and giving away what little money he had. He spent most of his time in his favorite coffee shop where he met young female prostitutes who apparently enjoyed his company and appreciated his concern for them. We were a world apart in that I represented someone whom the world would judge as successful, while he was labeled as inept and thus felt totally worthless.

I was not sure how I could help this man, but I tried to bolster his self-concept in some small way by suggesting an exercise. I said, "Antonio, pretend that you are sitting in that chair over there and that God is judging you. What good things can we say about that person? Is he good-hearted, sensitive, giving? Does he share unselfishly what he has? Is he kind to others? Is he honest; can he be trusted? Does he tend to be non-judgmental and accepting of other people?"

By the time we had gone through a half dozen traits, I began to feel distinctly more uncomfortable as I pondered whether, by God's measuring stick, I could compare favorably with this individual. I have continued to see Antonio sporadically over the years through many crises and hospitalizations, and I have never forgotten that I was not superior to him in God's eyes.

I learned an important rule in my work with violent youth, namely: "Whenever you see rage, look for the wound." And the wound usually consists of some form of self-hate that generates defensiveness and fear. Violence by men against women is often an expression of a painful sense of helplessness that is triggered unwittingly by the woman's "throwing salt" (as one man put it) on a deep, unhealed wound from the past. But, again, violence is a learned response to emotional pain. It was learned either from the example set by a man's father or by the father figures within his cultural circle.

A sense of helplessness and fear can trigger violence in almost any animal. The dehumanizing effects of our technological society tend to increase our sense of helplessness and fear, and the emotions of despair and rage become increasingly more difficult to contain. That crazed "animal in the basement" welcomes societies' permissible targets for attack: the order to "kill," whether it be for a "just war," "ethnic cleansing" or, as Monster Kody wrote *Monster*, (1993) "to protect the honor of his 'hood"(i.e., neighborhood).

Many people are frightened by their own rage which rises to the surface during arguments. Even a relatively healthy middle-class Caucasian woman, one who had always seen herself as well-composed and basically compliant, came to me confused and guilty because of her recently vicious arguments with her husband. I put her through the exercise "the animal in the basement," (page 130), and then showed her the cover of the book *Jelly Bean versus Dr. Jekyll & Mr. Hyde* (1989) reproduced here with the permission of M R K Publishing. She asked to have it copied and enlarged so she could put it on the wall in her kitchen for her husband's benefit. She used it to point out to him:

"THIS IS HOW YOU MAKE ME FEEL INSIDE WHEN YOU INVALIDATE ME!"

If we want to decrease the violence potential in a man or woman, we must decrease that person's sense of helplessness through empowerment, not by punishment. Here is where it is important to distinguish the difference between violence and aggression. Aggression in a man with a strong will-to-power is motivated by the intoxicating sense of self-aggrandizement and, if not properly channeled can result in the enjoyment of cruelty for its own sake.

On a grander scale, I believe that men such as Saddam Hussein are almost impossible to constrain, because they are not motivated primarily by selfishness but by a sense of historical purpose or mission. A more positive example, in my estimation, was general Charles de Gaulle, who came out of retirement and "volunteered" to become the president of France when that country desperately needed inspirational leadership. I remember reading an interesting statement he was quoted to have made: "I am only interested in de Gaulle from an historical perspective."

The world, at the time of this printing, is transfixed by the O.J. Simpson trial. I do not know whether or not O.J. physically participated in the crime for which he is accused, but I do know for certain that if we examine his inner spirit he is innocent, just as we all are innocent. It has taken me years to understand this concept. Fear permeates the planet Earth, compelling acts of selfishness and cruelty, and unless we can overcome guilt and self-hate there can be no end to violence.

It is important to maintain a sense of our spiritual purity separate from the instinctual impulses of our animal body, because it is impossible for our spiritual self to be a participant in a crime against another soul. It is as if we have an indwelling observing self that winces at the barbaric behavior of our programmed personality. I suspect that many of my readers have experienced this conflict. I see it as a prime cause of neurosis. I see patients every day whose mental distress can be traced to the conflict created by the difference between their true identity and the personality that their parents and society have imposed upon them. We are admonished, shortly after birth, to work hard to be "the best you can possibly be." What does this really mean? Would a tiger become the best tiger it could possibly be by joining a circus and learning to jump through hoops? What does our pet cat or pet dog have to do to earn our love? Must they constantly strive to be the best animal they can possibly be in order to earn our acceptance?

The world cannot diminish our essential lovableness or take away our innocence despite the dozens of small or major actions we feel compelled to commit against our inner sense of knowing better. Our true identity is more closely linked to our heart's desire than to our behavior. Until we learn to forgive ourselves we will continue to enjoy listening to gossip, making unkind judgments, and relishing the finding of guilt in others. On some level, many people hope that O.J. will be found innocent, just as we all want to be found innocent, ourselves, of the dozens of offenses we commit against our indwelling Self every day.

The fact that we are innocent on the spiritual level wherein our true identity lies does not excuse us from conforming to the rules of our society and accepting its proscribed punishments for lapses in our will, lapses which lead to acts of violence against others.

Anger is always a form of temporary insanity, a fear reaction of the animal body experiencing helplessness. If it is fed through obsessive thinking, it can overcome the restraints of the will and lead to unconscionable acts that later bring remorse. The O.J. Simpson case has served to call attention to the problem of family violence at all levels of society, violence that is too often dismissed with denial.

According to many ancient prophesies, the world is rapidly reaching a confrontational choice between the animal and the spiritual nature of humanity. Robert Lewis Stevenson had an enlightening dream regarding this battle within which he described in his classic novel *Dr. Jekyll &*

Mr. Hyde. None of us are immune from the Dr. Jekyll & Mr. Hyde syndrome. Dr. Jekyll became intrigued with the exhilaration and power he experienced when surrendering to the animal nature of Mr. Hyde. Eventually this behavior became an addiction that possessed the rational mind of Dr. Jekyll.

Albert Camus describes this conflict well in his play, *The Plague*:

"...each of us has the plague within him; no one, no one on earth is free from it. And I know, too, that we must keep endless watch on ourselves lest in a careless moment we breathe in somebody's face and fasten the infection on him. What's natural is the microbe. All the rest-—health, integrity, purity (if you like) is a product of the human will, of a vigilance that must never falter. The good man, the man who infects hardly anyone is the man who has the fewest lapses of attention. And it needs tremendous will power, a never-ending tension of the mind, to avoid such lapses."

It is the responsibility of all of us to keep our minds free from crippling negative emotions such as fear, worry, resentment, anger, jealousy, blame and guilt that are so commonly projected by the average person. Instead we must insist, by an act of will, upon fostering the healthy proactive emotions of praise, acceptance, appreciation, gratitude, joy, and love.

I believe that we can add meaning and purpose to our lives by viewing all of our experiences as necessary steps, in the evolutionary process of our learning, toward the expansion of our consciousness to ever higher levels of maturity and wisdom. As we see in nature, evolution involves a pattern of building up and tearing down and building up again. We live in a society that seeks quick solutions to problems. However, the evolutionary process is not one of final solutions, answers, or endings but of an unceasing, ever-shifting pattern of change and growth. From this context:

- How we work together is more important than what we produce.

- Relationship is more important than control through power.

- "Being" is more significant than doing, and

- NOW is more important than yesterday or tomorrow.

Acknowledgment

I want to acknowledge the contribution of William Meisterfeld, whose philosophy of *Mutual Respect* and *Training Without Pain* earned him the Canine Distinction Award for A.K.C. Obedience (1957) and National Retriever Championships for three consecutive years (1962, 1963, 1964), with a perfect 500 score in 1962. The idea of equating the training of a child with the methods used in properly training an animal, such as a dog, is somewhat novel and perhaps controversial, but nevertheless offers many worthwhile answers to a problem that has been made overly complicted in the psychiatric literature.